SYNOD OF SLEUTHS:
Essays on Judeo-Christian Detective Fiction

edited by
JON L. BREEN
and
MARTIN H. GREENBERG

The Scarecrow Press, Inc.
Metuchen, N.J., & London
1990

British Library Cataloguing-in-Publication data available

Library of Congress Cataloging-in-Publication Data

Synod of sleuths : essays on Judeo-Christian detective fiction / edited by Jon L. Breen and Martin H. Greenberg.
   p.   cm.
Includes bibliographical references and index.
ISBN 0-8108-2382-9 (acid-free paper)
1. Detective and mystery stories, English--History and criticism. 2. Detective and mystery stories, American--History and criticism. 3. Christian fiction--History and criticism. 4. Jewish fiction--History and criticism. 5. Clergy in literature. I. Breen, Jon L., 1943- . II. Greenberg, Martin Harry.
PR830.D4S96   1990
823'.087209382--dc20   90-21025

Copyright © 1990 by Jon L. Breen and Martin H. Greenberg
Manufactured in the United States of America
Printed on acid-free paper

Table of Contents

Introduction by Jon L. Breen	v
The Priestly Sleuths by Edward D. Hoch	1
Is This Any Job for a Nice Jewish Boy? (Jews in Detective Fiction) by James Yaffe	19
Protestant Mysteries by Jon L. Breen	57
Religious Cults and the Mystery by Marvin Lachman	79
Mormon Mysteries by Jon L. Breen	111
Religious Detective Fiction: A Symposium of Practitioners by Ellis Peters, William X. Kienzle, Harry Kemelman and Sister Carol Anne O'Marie	127
Bibliography	137
Index of Names	159

INTRODUCTION

by Jon L. Breen

It should not be surprising that works of mystery and detective fiction often draw on the world of religion for their backgrounds, their characters, their points of view, and even their detectives. A cynic could say the reason is that the history of religion has never lacked for the kind of malice and violence essential to a crime story. The more optimistic reason is that detective fiction is intrinsically the most moral kind of fiction, almost always involving--to some extent at least--a victory of good over evil. Whichever explanation you choose, the attraction of the field for readers and writers who have religious interests is not hard to understand.

Aside from the creators of overtly religious detective fiction most of this volume addresses, it might be interesting to enumerate some of the other connections between the fields. Some of the earliest examples of the mystery story are found in the *Apocrypha*, specifically *Bel and the Dragon* and *The Story of Susannah*, both anthologized as *The History of Bel* and *The History of Susannah* by Dorothy L. Sayers. In the genre's more recent history, a fair number of clergy have been practitioners, including Roman Catholic Monsignor Ronald A. Knox, Anglican Canon Victor L. Whitechurch, Anglican vicar Ivon Baker, and (among the writers covered in the various essays to follow) Rabbi Joseph Telushkin, Father Andrew Greeley, former priest William X. Kienzle, Methodist minister Charles Merrill Smith, and Sister Carol Anne O'Marie.

Consider, too, the number of lay religious writers who have contributed to the form, among them Dorothy L. Sayers, G. K. Chesterton, Fulton Oursler (as Anthony Abbott), and Catholic philosopher Ralph McInerny. In addition, a number of writers who have seldom written about religion overtly have been self-identified as religiously observant: Edmund Crispin, Michael Gilbert, Dorothy B. Hughes, Mildred and Gordon Gordon, Anthony Boucher, Edward D. Hoch, Jonathan Kellerman, Faye Kellerman, and undoubtedly many others. Among fans and analysts have been the Reverend Robert Washer, a Baptist pastor who edited a fanzine devoted to Ellery Queen in the late 1960s and early 1970s; Unitarian minister Maryell Cleary, who regularly contributes articles and reviews to various mystery journals; Erik Routely, once president of the Congregational Church in England and Wales and a prolific scholar in the fields of theology and church music, who wrote the provocative study, *The Puritan Pleasures of the Detective Story* (1972); and most recently theologian William David Spencer, author of the definitive work on religious detectives, *Mysterium and Mystery: The Clerical Crime Novel* (1989).

And what about the religious values of fictional detectives not specifically members of the clergy? Certainly Melville Davisson Post's Uncle Abner, who appears in eighteen stories in the 1918 volume bearing his name and four more in *The Methods of Uncle Abner* (1974), all collected in *The Complete Uncle Abner* (1977), constantly shares his religious perspective, making his adventures in Virginia of the 1820s the first American religious detective tales as well as the first series of historical detective stories. And at least one writer (Edgar S. Rosenberger) has argued persuasively that Sherlock Holmes himself was a strongly religious man--see the essay "The Religious Sherlock Holmes" (1948). Holmes' creator, Sir Arthur Conan Doyle, was, of course, a proponent of the

Spiritualist religion in his latter years, a viewpoint he never transferred to Holmes, though he did inflict it on his science-fictional hero Prof. Challenger in *The Land of Mist* (1926).

The decade just past has been noted (among other things) for a revival of interest in religion in the United States. Much of this revival has benefitted conservative evangelical Christianity at the expense of the so-called mainline Protestant denominations, and surely many of the most visible religious leaders of recent years have been televangelists, some most noted for political activism (Pat Robertson, Jerry Falwell), others for worldly failings (Jim Bakker, Jimmy Swaggart). The public evangelist has become a standard enough character in much recent detective fiction to fill many a sanctuary, though the number of sympathetic ones could be counted on the fingers of one hand.

In the essays that follow, several prominent author/critics of mystery fiction discuss various aspects of the interface between Judeo-Christian religion and detection. Edward D. Hoch, probably the all-time most prolific writer of detective short stories, numbers among his many series sleuths Father David Noone. In his essay, he surveys the large number of Catholic priests, nuns, and lay brothers among fictional detectives. James Yaffe, creator of the archetypal Jewish-mother detective known only as Mom, surveys Judaism and the mystery, not only covering the rabbi detectives but expanding into other depictions of Judaism and Jewish characters in mystery fiction. (These first two essays were written about three years ago and owe their non-currency to the failure of the first-named editor to get this volume ready for publication more quickly. Apologies are extended, and each essay has been appended with a brief summary of more recent developments.)

My own first contribution covers Protestant religious mysteries. Not attempting to cover all the fictional detectives from this branch of Christianity--they are ably covered in the Spencer volume frequently alluded to--I have concentrated on two writers, Charles Merrill Smith, the creator of Reverend Randollph, the closest Protestant equivalent to Father Brown and Rabbi Small, and Gaylord Larsen, illustrative of the specifically evangelical mystery novel without a clergy detective. Casting perhaps the largest and widest net is Marvin Lachman, surely one of the most capable and knowledgeable as well as *the* most prolific of mystery fan-critics, whose essay covers some of the many religious cults that have served as a background for mystery fiction. Finally, my second essay discusses the use of the Church of Jesus Christ of Latter-day Saints as a background for fictional detection.

A number of writers of religious detective stories were surveyed for their answers to a series of questions. Though the number of authors replying was somewhat disappointing, the content of their answers was not, and these are presented in the final section. While Ellis Peters and William X. Kienzle chose to answer each question individually, the responses of Harry Kemelman and Sister Carol Anne O'Marie are more general.

The bibliography lists a selection of books and articles about religion and the mystery plus all fictional works referred to in the book.

THE PRIESTLY SLEUTHS

by Edward D. Hoch

Who was the first Catholic priest to act as a detective in fiction?

Father Brown, of course.

It would be tempting to open this study of priests and nuns as fictional detectives with an entirely different answer, to say that Father Brown's appearance in 1910 was eight years too late, that the first priest detective was actually Father Michael Logan in a 1902 French play by Paul Anthelme (Paul Bourde) titled *Nos Deux Consciences* (*Our Two Consciences*).

I have not read the play in question, and I suspect that in the original French the priest's name was not Father Logan. But that was his name in the 1952 film adaptation by Alfred Hitchcock titled *I Confess*. On screen it was the story of a Quebec priest who hears a killer's confession and must keep sacred the seal of the confessional even when he himself is accused of the crime. Father Logan never functioned as a detective and the plot was resolved by another means entirely, although this early use of the confessional situation in suspense fiction or drama is worth noting. We'll see it many times again in various forms.

But the honor of being the first priest detective in fiction still belongs to G. K. Chesterton's Father Brown.

In the September 1910 issue of a British monthly called the *Storyteller*, the editor wrote, "Father Brown is a character destined to be long remembered in fiction." His words introduced the first of the Father Brown stories, "The Blue Cross," and he could not have imagined how true they would prove to be. Nearly eighty years later, Chesterton's character remains not only the first but certainly still the best of detective fiction's priestly sleuths.

The first collection of twelve stories, *The Innocence of Father Brown*, is not only the best of the five Father Brown books to appear between 1911 and 1935 but is arguably the best collection of detective short stories ever published. The level of excellence here, with only one or two weak stories among the dozen, is surely higher than in *The Adventures of Sherlock Holmes* with its mere handful of classics. Some of the early Father Brown stories like "The Sign of the Broken Sword" and "The Honour of Israel Gow" actually improve upon rereading and can be read any number of times without losing their compelling qualities. Even the more improbable tales in the book, like "The Secret Garden" and "The Invisible Man," mesmerize the reader with their ingenuity. Each reader seems to have his or her own favorite. Some pick "The Queer Feet" with its commentary upon the distinct classes of society. Others choose "The Blue Cross" or "The Hammer of God" or "The Eye of Apollo." Virtually every story in the book has become an anthology favorite.

What is the secret of Father Brown's success? What is it that places him, even now, head and shoulders above the other priest detectives who have followed in his footsteps? It is simply that Father Brown and his creator cared more about ideas than about facts. Indeed when we look through the text of "The Blue Cross" for the first recorded words out of Father Brown's mouth we find they are, ". . . what they really meant in the Middle Ages by the heavens being incorruptible." And Father Brown knows that the thief Flambeau is not a real priest because he attacks reason, which is bad theology. (By way of contrast, the first recorded words out of Nero Wolfe's mouth are, "Where's the beer?")

It is surprising to realize that Chesterton did not become a Roman Catholic until eleven years after the first Father Brown book. Of course he numbered Catholic priests among his friends, and his interest in the metaphysical had revealed itself even before Father Brown, in books like *The Man Who Was Thursday*. The Father Brown tales have rightly been called the first metaphysical detective stories, and perhaps that is one reason why they have never transferred with total success to films or television.

Father Brown's triumphs did not cease with his first twelve cases. Although the later books are somewhat uneven, each contains its high spots. In *The Wisdom of Father Brown* there are "The Man in the Passage" and "The Perishing of the Pendragons." In *The Incredulity of Father Brown*, a volume in which seven of the eight stories concern locked rooms or impossible crimes, we find "The Dagger With Wings" and perhaps the best Father Brown story of them all, "The Oracle of the Dog." Here Chesterton presents us with both an impossible murder and the seemingly supernatural behavior of a dog, with a cleverly constructed solution in which one explains the other. In a way it is one of his most religious stories, with a blending of paradox and puzzle that is uniquely Chestertonian.

The Father Brown stories were written quickly, like all of Chesterton's work, and usually when he needed money for some project. Much of the money from the last two volumes of stories went to finance *GK's Weekly*, a journal of economic, political and literary commentary that was his pet project during the last eleven years of his life. But these final volumes have their memorable stories too. *The Secret of Father Brown* offers "The Mirror of the Magistrate," one of two Father Brown tales in which the plot hinges upon characters failing to recognize themselves in dimly-lit mirrors. In the last collection, *The Scandal of Father Brown*, we find "The Green Man" and "The Blast of the Book," in which superstition is again defeated by the rational. A final story, "The Vampire of the Village," has Father Brown exposing a fake Anglican minister, just as in his first adventure he unmasked a false Catholic priest.

Certain of Chesterton's favorite themes can be traced through the fifty-one adventures of Father Brown. In addition to the paradoxes, the impostors and the mirrors which are often present, there is the idea of not noticing those of a lower social class who provide necessary but unappreciated services. Thus in various stories a waiter, a postman and a clerk are unnoticed or unrecognized. Chesterton made his points well, and his stories survive because of it.

Given the popularity of the Father Brown stories, it is surprising that several decades passed before there was another priest detective. Even Monsignor Ronald Knox, a Catholic priest turned mystery writer, used no clerical sleuth in his half-dozen novels and single short story. It was not until thirty years after Father Brown's first appearance that another member of the Catholic clergy appeared as a fictional sleuth, and then it was not a priest but a nun.

Anthony Boucher's *Nine Times Nine*, originally published in 1940 under the name "H. H. Holmes," is a novel that Chesterton would have loved. Sister Ursula of the fictional order Martha of Bethany is a character very much like Father Brown. We first meet her as she finishes counseling a young girl who wishes to enter the order. The first words we hear from her lips are, "Yes, I have finally talked that silly child out of becoming a nun."

Readers of *Nine Times Nine* will recognize the paradox, the bogus cult at the Temple of Light, the locked-room murder, and the erudite conversation elements as that Chesterton loved to use. In fact, if Chesterton had ever written a Father Brown novel it probably would have been quite a bit like *Nine Times Nine*. The novel remains Anthony Boucher's best effort.

Sister Ursula appeared in one other novel, *Rocket to the Morgue* (1942), in which she becomes involved with a locked-room murder and other killings among a group of science-fiction writers and fans. The novel reflects Boucher's interest in science fiction and his friendship with numerous science fiction writers, some of whom served as the basis for characters in the book. As a Sister Ursula mystery, however, it is inferior to *Nine Times Nine*.

Sister Ursula also appeared in three short stories. One of them, "The Stripper," contains an interesting clue making use of the ecclesiastic calendar of the Catholic Church. Catholic themes continued to appear in some of Boucher's science fiction writing, but two novels and three short stories are all that we have of Sister Ursula. It's a pity.

Perhaps the first mystery-suspense novel with a Catholic priest functioning as a detective remains to this day one of the very best. It is *A Gentle Murderer* by Dorothy Salisbury Davis, published in 1951. It is not a whodunit, and the reader knows from the beginning that a gentle young man named Tim Brandon committed the murder about which he told Father Duffy in the darkness of the confessional booth. But the priest functions as a real detective as he puts together clues from Brandon's childhood in an attempt to find the man before he kills again. A detective named Sergeant Goldsmith is on the same trail, not trying to save a soul but only to catch a murderer.

Sadly, Father Duffy never reappeared in the novels of Dorothy Salisbury Davis, although a more modern sort of priest, Father McMahon, solves the mystery in another of her novels, *Where the Dark Streets Go* (1969).

It's possible that Davis' use of Father Duffy and Sergeant Goldsmith to track down the killer in *A Gentle Murderer* might have inspired another writer, Jack Webb (no relation to the television actor-director), to team up a Catholic priest and a Jewish detective sergeant a year later in *The Big Sin* (1952), the first of a nine-book series. Sergeant Sammy Golden usually played a larger part in the investigations than Father Joseph Shanley, although Webb seemed more at ease with the Catholic background of Shanley than with the lightly sketched Jewishness of Golden.

The nine Shanley-Golden novels met with mixed critical reception, possibly because there was a certain sameness to their plots involving a number of separate cases and incidents which come together at the end. Anthony Boucher, reviewing mysteries for *The New York Times*, had praised *A Gentle Murderer* as "The year's most distinguished blend of a compassionate straight novel with a formal detective story," but he never listed any of the Webb series among his favorites. *The Big Sin* remains the best of the series, followed by *The Brass Halo* (1957) and *The Deadly Sex* (1959).

The only nun detective to appear between Sister Ursula and the 1980s was Soeur Angele in three French

The Priestly Sleuths 7

novels by Henri Catalan, beginning with *Soeur Angele and the Embarrassed Ladies* (1955). The books attracted little general attention when English translations were brought out by the Catholic publisher Sheed & Ward, and they are all but forgotten today. Earlier, the same firm published Eric Shepherd's *Murder in a Nunnery* and *More Murder in a Nunnery*, the first of which became a frequently produced play in Catholic schools. In both cases, however, the mysteries are solved by Superintendent Pearson of Scotland Yard and not by a nun.

In 1959 the Irish-American journalist Leonard Wibberley, best known for his humorous novel *The Mouse That Roared*, began producing a series of mystery novels under the pseudonym of Leonard Holton. There would be eleven in all over the next eighteen years, with Father Joseph Bredder as the continuing sleuth. A Franciscan priest who served with the marines in World War II, Bredder is chaplain of the Convent of the Holy Innocent in Los Angeles, and in his cases he usually shares the spotlight with Lieutenant Minardi of the LAPD.

First of the Father Bredder novels, and still one of the best, is *The Saint Maker* (1959), in which the serial killer chooses victims recently absolved of their sins, believing he is sending them to Heaven. The head of one victim is found before a statue of John the Baptist in Father Bredder's church. This was quickly followed by *A Pact With Satan* (1960), about a woman who believes her dead husband is trying to burn her alive, and *Secret of the Doubting Saint* (1961), about a television producer and a missing diamond. In the fourth book, *Deliver Us From Wolves* (1963), Father Bredder investigates the apparent presence of werewolves in a Portuguese village.

Later Bredder novels deal with specific interests of the author, such as a California to Hawaii yacht race in *A Touch of Jonah* (1968), a rare violin in *A Problem of Angels* (1970), and professional baseball in *The Devil to Play* (1973). All are worth reading, though the later books lack some of the freshness of the first Bredder adventures. This priest detective is at his best when focusing on spiritual concerns, as he often does. Many of the books contain a criminal plot running parallel with Father Bredder's clerical activities, thus somewhat anticipating the later Rabbi Small novels of Harry Kemelman.

Mention should be made here of a 1961 anthology, *Bodies and Souls*, edited by Dan Herr and Joel Wells. Published as a part of Doubleday's Crime Club series and billed as a collection of thrilling tales with Catholic settings, mood or characters, the book offers only Father Brown among clerical sleuths. Several of the fourteen tales are ghost stories, and others have only a passing connection with Catholicism. Best of the lot is Frank Ward's detective novelette "The Dark Corner," about the murder of a priest in his confessional. Although Father Brett plays a large part in the action, the mystery is mainly solved by Lieutenant Archer of the police.

During the 1960s and early 1970s, priests in the role of detective were more likely to turn up in short stories than in novels, except for the Holton novels mentioned above. A long-running series of short mysteries about Father Crumlish, created by Alice Scanlan Reach, got underway with "In the Confessional" in the June 1962 issue of *Ellery Queen's Mystery Magazine.* Interestingly enough this story, which won a prize as the "best first" in an *EQMM* contest, is told from the point of view of a church thief named Blue who hides in the confessional and overhears a young man confess to the recent murder of a choir girl at the church. Father Crumlish is a secondary character and does not solve the mystery contained in his first case.

It was not until "The Ordeal of Father Crumlish" in the April 1963 issue of *EQMM* that the priest of St. Brigid's Church, now fully identified as Father Francis Xavier Crumlish, emerged as a full-fledged sleuth, solving the knifing death of a parish youth at the church's annual field day festival. There are some thirteen Father Crumlish stories in all.

The year 1964 marked the appearance of the first of three stories about Father David Noone by Edward D. Hoch. The first two have been described as "rather feeble" by Francis M. Nevins, Jr., but Father Noone improved somewhat with his third case, "The Sweating Statue," in which he was helped to the solution by Monsignor Thomas Xavier. It appears in a 1985 anthology *Detectives A to Z*, edited by Frank D. McSherry, Jr., Martin H. Greenberg and Charles G. Waugh.

In the late 1970s novels about priest detectives seemed once more in favor. One of the most successful series began in 1977 with Ralph McInerny's *Her Death of Cold*, about parish priest Father Roger Dowling. The Irish-Catholic McInerny is a former seminarian who has taught at the University of Notre Dame since 1955 and is now a Professor of Philosophy there. He has authored several books of moral philosophy and at least five on the life and thoughts of St. Thomas Aquinas.

The middle-aged Father Dowling is a former alcoholic, the pastor and only priest at St. Hilary's Church, an out-of-the-way parish in Fox River, west of Chicago. Part of the charm of the Dowling books is their wealth of secondary characters. Dowling's old seminary classmate, Captain Keegan, the rectory housekeeper, Marie Murkin, Lieutenant Horvath and a black police officer, Agnes Lamb (in the later books), all play their parts.

Like the best of continuing series, the Father Dowling books have improved over the years. After a good beginning in *Her Death of Cold*, about the murder of an elderly, unloved woman, the next few Dowling novels proved uneven. *The Seventh Station* (1977), about a mad priest, is interesting, if complicated, and *Bishop as Pawn* (1978), about broken marriages and a kidnapped bishop, contains strong statements of the author's own beliefs. But *Lying Three* (1979) is routine and *Second Vespers* (1981), about a supposedly dead author in Fox River, is not as good as it should be, despite McInerny's admirable attempt to make discussions of Catholic doctrine a better-integrated part of the plot.

There is no general agreement about the best of the Father Dowling books, but there seems to be a decided improvement beginning with *Thicker Than Water* (1981). A 1983 book, *The Grass Widow*, about a woman who dies after being threatened by her estranged husband on his disc jockey radio show, may be the best to date, although the 1984 book *Getting a Way With Murder*, about an acquitted wife-murderer, is also good. Taking the series as a whole, Father Dowling must be judged superior to Father Bredder and the best priest detective to emerge since Father Brown. No single Dowling book, however, is as good as William X. Kienzle's *The Rosary Murders* (1979), the first of the Father Koesler series.

Kienzle is himself a former priest, and his priestly sleuth is virtually a duplicate of himself, sharing the same physical description and the same background in the Detroit Catholic diocese. He makes a point of avoiding depictions of troubled priests, and none ever suffer the conflicts which caused the author himself to leave the priesthood. In *The Rosary Murders* Father Robert Koesler must track down a serial killer who chooses priests and nuns as his

The Priestly Sleuths

victims and leaves a rosary with each body. As with several of the earlier books we've discussed, important information comes to Father Koesler in the confessional, and he is placed in the classic dilemma.

If *The Rosary Murders* is the best of the nine Koesler mysteries to date, the young priest's second case, *Death Wears a Red Hat*, is almost as good, with its overtones of voodoo and another string of bizarre killings. This time the decapitated heads of the victims (reminding us of a scene from Leonard Holton's *The Saint Maker*) are found on headless statues in Detroit churches. The author even takes time for a little inside joke, with the brief appearance of a priest named "Father McInerny."

By the third novel, *Mind Over Murder* (1981), about a missing and disliked monsignor, we begin to notice an oddity about William Kienzle's series. Is the author obsessed with the letter K? In addition to Father Koesler and another continuing character, Inspector Koznicki, we find ourselves with characters named Harry Kirwan and Nelson Kane. It is a long book, like many of the Father Koesler mysteries, and some readers will find the solution both disappointing and unsatisfactory. A later novel, *Kill and Tell* (1984), offers another variation on the confessional plot. This time Father Koesler and Inspector Koznicki are joined by characters named Bill Kelly and Al Kirkus.

There are other jarring notes in the later books, like a bit too much slapstick humor in *Assault With Intent* (1982), and bizarre plotting involving the Mafia, the Rastafarians and a seeming attempt to destroy the papacy in *Shadow of Death* (1983). Touches of the supernatural intrude in some of the books. Still, Kienzle's writing is usually witty and urbane, his portraits of the priests and nuns of Detroit are lovingly drawn, as are those of his continuing secondary characters, Inspector Koznicki, black

Lieutenant Ned Harris, and a pair of reporters who are also lovers, Joe Cox and Pat Lennon. Pat Lennon plays an especially important part in *Death Wears a Red Hat*.

We keep reading William Kienzle's books because we know he is capable of writing a mystery as good as, or even better than, *The Rosary Murders*. So far it hasn't come. Among the most recent books, *Sudden Death* (1985) dealt with the murder of a pro football player, while *Deadline For a Critic* (1987) was about the killing of a bisexual theater and music critic, told mainly through a long flashback about his life. There is virtually no detection by Father Koesler and the ending again disappoints our expectations.

Not content with his annual Father Dowling novels, Ralph McInerny began a second series of mysteries in 1981, using the pseudonym of "Monica Quill"—a real pen name! With *Not a Blessed Thing!* he introduced nun detective Sister Mary Teresa who went on to star in a series with punning titles like *Let Us Prey* (1982) and *And Then There Was Nun* (1984).

Like the Dowling books, the series started well, faltered a bit, and then recovered nicely. Sister Mary Teresa Dempsey is short, fat and ancient, a believer in the old ways of the church who lives with two younger sisters—all that remain of her order. Sister Kim's brother Richard is on the Chicago police force, and it is Sister Kim who does much of the legwork in the novels while Sister Mary Teresa remains at home, not unlike Nero Wolfe. In *Let Us Prey*, the third nun, Sister Joyce, involves them in the strangulation murders of a number of young neighborhood women. A radio station and an organization for divorced women figure strongly in the plot. The third book is probably the best of the series so far. The plot of *And Then There Was Nun* revolves around women's soccer, with the team's director and top star among the victims.

Later books in the series, *Nun of the Above* (1985) and *Sine Qua Nun* (1986), hold up well. In the latter, Sister Mary Teresa actually appears on a local television show where she meets a novelist infamous for his thinly-disguised portraits of real people. He's soon murdered, and there are lots of suspects.

The Monica Quill books are not perfect. Occasionally the reader may be annoyed by the constant references to Sister Mary Teresa as "Emtee," from her initials. And the gathering of the suspects for the final confrontation scene seems a bit old-fashioned, a fault Quill shares with the Nero Wolfe novels. When an author creates a detective who rarely leaves home, the options for an ending are distinctly limited. Still, the idea of three nuns from a defunct order teaming up to investigate crimes has its charms, and the net result is another winner for Ralph McInerny.

Only one other nun detective was to appear during the early 1980s, but Sister Mary Helen's cases are unique in that they are written by an actual nun, Sister Carol Anne O'Marie. *A Novena For Murder*, Sister Mary Helen's first case, tells how the 75-year-old nun retires to Mount St. Francis College for Women in San Francisco, only to be confronted with an earthquake and a murdered professor. Police Inspectors Kate Murphy and Dennis Gallegher are on hand to investigate, but when a second murder occurs Sister Mary Helen finds she must lend them a hand. The series continues in good form, most recently with *Advent of Dying* (1986).

Sister Mary Helen is the last of the nun detectives to date unless one wishes to include ex-nun Bridget O'Toole in Frank McConnell's *Murder Among Friends*. If none of them quite measure up to Anthony Boucher's Sister Ursula, they are still pleasant and diverting company.

The most recent of the priest detectives is Father Blackie Ryan, who has appeared to date in five novels by Andrew M. Greeley, himself a Catholic priest. He is the first practicing priest to create a fictional priest detective, and the evolution of Blackie Ryan takes some explaining. After four bestselling mainstream novels (and a 1980 suspense novel he likes to forget), Father Greeley created Blackie Ryan as the principal character in his 1985 novel *Virgin and Martyr*. The Chicago priest investigates the torture killing of a religious young woman in Latin America, and comes to some startling conclusions. The irony of the title is clear only at the book's end. Father Blackie Ryan certainly functions as a detective in his first appearance, and the book must be considered his best case to date.

It was followed in 1986 by *Angels of September*, in which Blackie Ryan becomes a secondary but still important character. The novel can best be described as dealing with a haunted art gallery in downtown Chicago. It is suspenseful and downright terrifying at times, but the ending (which may owe something to the film *Ghostbusters*) is purely supernatural. In a third Ryan novel, *Patience of a Saint*, the main character is a Chicago newspaper columnist. Although crime and murder play a part in the action, Blackie is reduced to a minor role.

In the meantime, however, Andrew Greeley launched a series of Blackie Ryan mystery novels, with the Chicago priest now promoted to Monsignor. He plans to publish eight titles in all, each based on one of the Beatitudes. Thus far two have appeared, *Happy Are the Meek* (1985) and *Happy Are the Clean of Heart* (1986). These are traditional detective stories, and the first even features a floor plan and a fairly clever locked room mystery, with mention of ghosts and a devil-worship cult on the very first page. It's a good, entertaining book, although the second in the series is not quite so successful. One gets the feeling that Blackie Ryan's best case will remain the mainstream novel *Virgin and Martyr.*

A final word should be added about two detectives who are neither priests nor nuns but still deserve mention here. They are Brother Cadfael and Brother William of Baskerville, both medieval monks whose detections take place in a monastic setting. Though they are lay brothers rather than ordained priests, one might argue that the books have a more distinctly religious flavor than is to be found in the modern cases of our urban priestly sleuths.

Brother Cadfael, a 12th Century Benedictine at the abbey of Saint Peter and Saint Paul in Shrewsbury, England, is the creation of British mystery writer Ellis Peters, a pseudonym of Edith Pargeter. The Edgar-winning author had sixteen previous mystery novels to her credit before she created Brother Cadfael in *A Morbid Taste For Bones* (1977), still one of the best of the series. It deals with a pilgrimage to acquire the bones of an obscure saint from a small Welsh village, a mission that leads to murder. After barely ten years the series now totals more than a dozen books.

Among the other notable Brother Cadfael titles are *Monk's-Hood* (1980), about the poisoning of a wealthy landowner; *The Leper of Saint Giles* (1981), about a romantic triangle and the murder whose trail leads to a nearby leper house; *The Virgin in the Ice* (1982), another series standout, about murder during the winter of England's civil war; *The Devil's Novice* (1983) and *Dead Man's Ransom* (1984). Not surprisingly, some of the later books have strayed far afield of monastic life, into more temporal troubles, but the series remains an interesting one.

Brother William of Baskerville, a 14th Century Franciscan visiting an abbey in the north of Italy, is the creation of the Italian novelist Umberto Eco and has appeared in only one book, the worldwide bestseller *The Name of the Rose* (1980, English edition 1983). Brother William investigates a series of bizarre murders at the monastery, having to do with secret manuscripts and a mysterious maze-like library. The lengthy book of more than 500 pages has been found a bit slow by some readers, but it remains a stunning success, both as a historical novel and a detective story.

Father Brown was the first, and I venture to predict that Monsignor Blackie Ryan will not be the last of the priest detectives. In their own way, priests and nuns combat evil as much as police officers and private detectives. As Chesterton's Father Brown pointed out in his first adventure, "Has it never struck you that a man who does next to nothing but hear men's real sins is not likely to be wholly unaware of human evil?"

* * *

EDITOR'S NOTE: Since this essay was written, there have been several developments regarding the Roman-Catholic detective story. A newly discovered Father Brown story, "The Donnington Affair," begun by Max Pemberton and completed by Chesterton in a magazine stunt, was reprinted for the first time in book form in a Chesterton collection called *Thirteen Detectives*. Edward D. Hoch and the co-editor of the present volume, Martin H. Greenberg, have collaborated on a new anthology of Catholic detectives stories, *Murder Most Sacred* (1989), which includes a noncomprehensive but useful bibliography of Catholic detective fiction. And several of the Catholic religious sleuths referred to continue to add new cases.

The Priestly Sleuths 17

Father Blackie Ryan appears in the third of Greeley's beatitudes series, *Happy are Those Who Thirst for Justice* (1987). Ralph McInerny's latest Father Dowling book is the novelette collection *Four on the Floor* (1989), while Sister Mary Teresa's most recent outing is *The Veil of Ignorance* (1988), published under McInerny's Monica Quill *nom de plume*. William X. Kienzle's Father Koesler continues his crime-solving career in *Eminence* (1989) and *Masquerade* (1990). Ellis Peters' Brother Cadfael has his most recent eleventh-century cases (#16 and 17) in *The Heretic's Apprentice* and *The Potter's Field* (both 1989).

In 1990, two additional Catholic religious sleuths made their debuts: Bishop Francis Regan in William F. Love's *The Chartreuse Clue* and Veronica Black's Sister Joan in *A Vow of Silence*.

IS THIS ANY JOB FOR A NICE JEWISH BOY?

(Jews in Detective Fiction)

by James Yaffe

The first detective in Western literature is God. And in His first case, recorded in the Book of Genesis, Chapter 3, He solves the primal crime from which, we are told, all future crimes have flowed.

The criminals are Adam and Eve. Having disobeyed God's injunction against eating the fruit of the Tree of Knowledge, they feel shame and cover themselves with fig leaves. God asks them why, and Adam replies, "I heard thy voice in the garden, and I was afraid, because I was naked; and I hid myself." Instantly God seizes on the key discrepancy in Adam's words: the knowledge of nakedness could have come to him only as a result of eating the fruit. "Who told thee that thou wast naked?" God says, and then visits on Adam and Eve the punishment which has caused their descendants so much trouble through the ages.

In this tale, going back to the beginnings of our culture, God's neat demonstration of logical deduction sets the pattern for all those later, more elaborate deductions that have delighted readers since Poe invented the detective story. And this is no accident. It is not difficult to see parallels between the attitudes and beliefs of Judaism, as expressed in the Old Testament and the underlying assumptions of the detective story thousands of years later.

First, traditional Judaism places primary

importance on human justice. Because the afterlife is not guaranteed—it is a mystery, Jews are told, that human beings cannot understand and are not supposed to be concerned with—justice here and now, in this world, is what matters.

Secondly, doing justice is inseparable from bringing out the truth, exposing the guilty and clearing the innocent: therefore it depends on evidence. God Himself, though in a mystical sense He knows all and sees all, has no right to make accusations without hard incontrovertible evidence, which must be based on facts, on the probabilities of human nature, and on logical deduction.

Finally, the Biblical story illustrates the pleasure Jews have always taken in argument and analysis. They love to weigh probabilities, to look at every side of every question, to solve puzzles—yes, sometimes to split hairs. Disputation, based on the logical interpretation of evidence, proves to Jews that they are human and made in God's image.

This love of argument is most clearly embodied in the Talmud, the great collection of rabbinical commentaries on the Torah, which was produced between the first and sixth centuries A.D. In the Talmud, distinguished rabbis meticulously, earnestly, but almost joyously take apart Biblical passages and pull out every subtle nuance of meaning from them. There is hardly any aspect of human thought and behavior—and especially of law—that the Talmud does not examine.

Given these ancient preoccupations, we might suppose that Jews would have taken early on to writing detective stories. But the historical fact is quite different. Many Jews may have read detective stories from the beginning, but during the so-called Golden Age of the form, roughly from the 1890s to

Is This Any Job for a Nice Jewish Boy?

the outbreak of World War II, few Jews wrote detective stories and there were no Jewish detective heroes.[1]

The reason for the dearth of Jewish detectives in the Golden Age is, I think, primarily social. The essential snobbishness of almost all detective stories during the first fifty years of the form's development has been remarked on by many critics, from Auden to Orwell to Colin Watson. The typical detective hero of this period moves in the highest classes of society, which of course is where the most interesting murders occur. He is Lord Peter Wimsey or Albert Campion (younger son of a noble mother); even Sherlock Holmes, we are told, has aristocratic forebears. Police officers of this period, if they are permitted to have intelligence and crime-solving abilities, often have aristocratic forebears too, like Ngaio Marsh's Roderick Alleyn. At any rate, they are always gentlemen, capable of holding their own socially and educationally in the bloody drawing rooms and libraries to which their duty calls them.

Whatever the reasons for the detectival snobbishness, much of it traveled across the Atlantic and settled on the American detective story of those

---

[1]None that I have been able to find, that is. Research on this subject is difficult. No official list of fictional Jewish detectives has ever been compiled, and most detective stories go out of print rather quickly. To discover every single example of the genre would take much more time than has been available for this brief survey. What follows, then, should be considered as a preliminary exploration, a skimming of the surface, a quick though enthusiastic introduction to the subject. I hope it will be useful for casual readers, and will inspire a few less casual ones to dig deeper.

same decades. There were some odd populist manifestations, like Melville Davisson Post's backwoods detective Uncle Abner, but these had very little influence; the great majority of American detectives, between the two World Wars, imitated their English counterparts slavishly, clipping their g's, peering at suspects through monocles, and making expert comments about wines, in the manner of Philo Vance, the most popular and insufferable of the lot.

Obviously, in this suffocatingly uppercrust social milieu, there was no room for Jewish detective heroes, and nobody knew it better than Jewish writers. The best of the Golden Age American detective characters, Ellery Queen, was created by two Jewish writers, Frederic Dannay and Manfred Lee; yet Ellery, though he lives at home with his police inspector father and in a way has gone into the family business, is never identified as Jewish. Indeed, in the earlier books he is described as wearing a pince-nez, very much in the Lord Peter style.

During this same period, of course, there was a radically different development in the American detective story—the school of hard-boiled fiction published in *Black Mask* magazine and producing its masterpieces in the novels of Dashiell Hammett. This school was a deliberate reaction against the genteel snobbery of the English upperclass detective story, but it did nothing to create a receptive atmosphere for the Jewish detective. In fact, the hard-boiled school was even less receptive, because it thrived on violence rather than logic; its heroes solved crimes with their guns, not with their reasoning powers. Talmudic rabbis can argue at the top of their lungs, but they are not supposed to pull guns on each other.

All in all, then, if there were no Jewish detectives in the 20s and 30s, it was probably because Jews felt too insecure in the society around them to

Is This Any Job for a Nice Jewish Boy? 23

try and impose their manners and mores on a popular literary form. And if this state of affairs has changed in the last three or four decades, if Jewish detectives have made more frequent appearances, it is probably because Jewish self-confidence has increased since the end of World War II. The revelations of the Holocaust, the establishment of the state of Israel, the growth of ecumenicism, and other factors have created an atmosphere in which Jewish detectives—along with Jewish college professors, Jewish movie stars, Jewish pop singers, and many other phenomena largely unknown before the war—can thrive.

The first fullfledged Jewish detective—at least that I have been able to discover—does not appear in a novel or a story at all. He is Moe Finkelstein, the New York Jewish policeman who is assigned to guard the Nazi consulate in the late Claire Boothe's 1940 play, *Margin for Error*. Ms. Booth—later the wife of Henry Luce and a figure of some importance in Republican politics—was not Jewish, but she produces a thoroughly authentic re-creation of the rhythms of Finkelstein's language, his stoical sense of irony at the job he's been saddled with, and the oddly Talmudic twists and turns of his mind as he solves the consul's murder. *Margin for Error* not only works well as a detective story—its clues are plentiful and fair, its solution is both surprising and, once you see it, inescapable—but paves the way for the Jewish detectives of the postwar years.

* * *

The most substantial of these is unquestionably Harry Kemelman's Rabbi David Small. Kemelman's hero, the spiritual leader of a small congregation in Barnard's Crossing, Massachusetts, is a short, unprepossessing young man, scholarly by nature and always uncomfortable in the jungle of congregational life. His cases are recounted in nine books, the first of which, *Friday the Rabbi Slept Late*, appeared in 1964. Six more books, each playing with the name of a day of the week, appeared in the next fourteen years; then, with the week over, there was a seven-year hiatus, until 1985 when Kemelman returned to Rabbi Small with *Someday the Rabbi Will Leave*. Yet another chapter in the series, *One Fine Day the Rabbi Bought a Cross*, has been published since then.

The Kemelman books are grounded in Judaism and Jewishness. In each one Rabbi Small encounters a murder and solves it through the application of Talmudic reasoning, using some specific Talmudic story or point of law as an analogy to explain his solution. At the same time, running parallel to the murder case, a problem arises in the rabbi's synagogue, usually one which could cause him to be voted out of his job by a hostile board or to quit over some point of religious principle. At the end of the book, the two strands inevitably come together. Often the solution of the murder case, which has drawn in several members of the rabbi's own congregation, brings about the solution of his synagogual problem.

Sometimes this neatness seems a bit mechanical, but it serves an important purpose, in allowing Kemelman to do two things at the same time. First, it allows him to deal with many of the most vital issues of American Jewish life—inter-marriage, anti-Semitism, the defection of young people from the synagogue, the balance between ritual observance and ethical behavior. Sometimes the rabbi delivers little lectures on these matters—just a bit too pedantically perhaps—but mostly they come to us embodied in accurate, vital, and highly entertaining pictures of contemporary American Jewish society. In the best tradition of realistic social-comedy novels from Jane Austen to Sinclair Lewis, Kemelman has a voracious appetite for detail. Nothing is too commonplace to capture his imagination and arouse his fascinated amusement. He notices, and sees the precise social significance of, what people wear and eat, how they furnish their homes, how they bring up their children, how they bury their dead, how they reconcile their religious commitments to their business practices. And his ear is uncanny: he catches the exact speech mannerisms of all his characters; none of his middleclass smalltown Jews sound exactly like any of the others. (His gentile characters are accurately depicted too, but never with the verve and sparkle that he brings to his Jews.)

At the same time, the parallel structure of the Rabbi Small novels allows Kemelman to integrate his social observation into the detective story plot. He clearly loves Talmudic logic—and detective stories as well—so he never makes us feel that his pictures of Jewish life are what he really cares about, and that he has simply grafted them onto the detective story form for the sake of convenience and bestsellerdom.

It will be clear, then, that the best of the Rabbi Small books are those in which the two central elements—the ingenious detective plot, with its Talmudic unraveling, and the sharp social observation—genuinely work together. This happens most successfully, I think, in the first of the books, *Friday the Rabbi Slept Late*, where the premises of the whole series are laid down through one lovely touch after another; in *Saturday the Rabbi Went Hungry*, in which the solution to the murder hinges on differences between Jewish and gentile drinking habits; and in *Wednesday the Rabbi Got Wet*, in which both the mystery and the rabbi's synagogual problem cast different lights on the question of how religion, in our world of extremism, is to walk the fine line between fanaticism and atheism.

In some of the other books, one element is strong and the other weak. In *Tuesday the Rabbi*

Saw Red an ingeniously worked-out crime and solution are undermined by the college setting Kemelman has chosen for them. His sense of what a college is like is peculiar, to say the least, and his pictures of unaffiliated Jewish youth are unconvincing. In *Someday the Rabbi Will Leave*, another good plot is spoiled by a rather tired rerun of the rabbi's struggle against a businessman chairman of his board. It was all done much more thoroughly and sharply in the very first book. In *Sunday the Rabbi Stayed Home* the Jewish social parts of the book are up to Kemelman's highest standard, particularly his picture of a fight between two factions in the synagogue; but the murder plot is tired and obvious, and Talmudic reasoning scarcely enters in at all, as if the author were losing interest in the very thing that gives these books their originality and power as detective stories.

The least successful of the Rabbi Small books are *Monday the Rabbi Took Off*, *Thursday the Rabbi Walked Out*, and the most recent, *One Fine Day the Rabbi Bought a Cross*. In *Monday* and once again in *One Fine Day*, Kemelman transports Rabbi Small to Israel for a vacation. The rabbi's observations of the differences between American and Israeli Jewish life are interesting, but in both books the Israeli characters are mostly stock types, and the plots are halfhearted melanges of Arab terrorism and Israeli secret-service heroics. In *Thursday*, the synagogual sections are distorted by Kemelman's simplistic and humorless treatment of Women's Lib, and the crime and its solution are grindingly obvious.

One weakness, common to all of the Rabbi Small books, prevents Kemelman from being quite in the league of an Austen or a Sinclair Lewis. A strain of sentimentality consistently mars the toughmindedness of his work. He is too prone to let his Jews off the hook because they <u>are</u> Jews, to smooth over unpleasant or tragic implications of their behavior.

Is This Any Job for a Nice Jewish Boy? 27

Rabbi Small's explanations of Jewish thought sometimes degenerate into rather complacent apologies. Judaism seems to have no faults, no limitations; any troubling questions it may raise are always explained away.

A symptom of this sentimentality is that in the nine books only twice does the murderer turn out to be a Jew. And in one of these instances the murder is self-defense, in the other an accident.

Nevertheless, despite this unevenness, Kemelman's achievement cannot be denied. In David Small he has created a truly original and enjoyable detective hero. In his combination of diffidence and stubbornness, integrity and almost childish impracticality, Rabbi Small is both admirable and exasperating, noble and absurd—as the greatest fictional detectives from Holmes through Poirot have been.

In order to fully appreciate the Kemelman books, we need only turn to Joseph Telushkin's *The Unorthodox Murder of Rabbi Wahl*, the first in a projected new series featuring another rabbi-detective, Daniel Winter. There is no reason, of course, why more than one rabbi-detective should not flourish. Rabbi Small's congregation of Conservative, Eastern, semi-suburban synagogue-goers represents only one segment, and not necessarily the largest, of the Jewish world in America. Telushkin's Daniel Winter leads a very different kind of congregation. It is located in Los Angeles and consists of wealthy sophisticated people, and the murder victim is a <u>female</u> rabbi (who could imagine such a thing in Barnard's Crossing?) who is also a militant feminist.

Winter himself is the antithesis of David Small. He is tall, dashing, "almost handsome"—which, in the code-language of romance fiction, is somehow even sexier and more glamorous than "handsome." He is also a media celebrity: he has written a successful book about Judaism, and he is the MC of a radio talk show. As in Kemelman's books, Telushkin counterpoints the murder his rabbi solves with problems in his private and synagogual life, but the problems are: should he allow himself to fall in love with a beautiful female police officer, and should he give up his job in his temple to become full-time host of a popular national talkshow?

These "problems" are the chief symptoms of what is wrong with Telushkin's book. Daniel Winter is hardly a character at all; he is a collection of wish-fulfillment fantasies that belong to the vulgarest contemporary notions about success and glamor. He has no individual personality, no real inner life, no sharply observed social world in which he moves; everything he thinks, feels, and struggles with comes out of the dead clichés of nighttime TV soap opera. He is Blake Carrington with a Talmudic education.

And Telushkin never seems to realize what a selfrighteous heavyhanded bore his hero is. Especially annoying is Telushkin's habit of sticking fulsome praises of the rabbi into the mouths of other characters: "Rabbi, I have to tell you something. As you led us out of the hall just now, the dean of the colleges grabbed me for a second and . . . he said this was the most beautiful service he'd ever attended."

The best thing about the book is its detective plot: Telushkin has created an interesting puzzle, with good clues and a genuinely surprising solution that is also logical. But it might have been embodied in a short story: it is simply not worth the effort of wading through 180 pages of pedestrian writing, flabby characterization, and the intolerably smug superiority of Rabbi Winter.

Another and totally different world of religious

Judaism is portrayed in Faye Kellerman's *The Ritual Bath*. Her setting is also Los Angeles, but the talk shows, celebrities, and media rabbis could not be farther away. Her heroine, Rina Lazarus, is a young widow who lives and works in a highly insular Orthodox Jewish community—almost a commune. Rina is in charge of the ritual bathhouse, in which the women of the community engage in regular rites of purification. Into this setting of peculiar intimacy and holiness, rape and murder intrude, and Rina finds herself drawn into the case and ultimately involved in solving it along with the police detective, Peter Decker, who has been assigned to it. Romantic feelings develop between Rina and Decker, and eventually he turns out to be a Jew, whose Jewishness has been hidden not only from the world but from himself.

This love affair is the weakest element in the book. Decker's secret Jewishness is fortuitous; it gives Rina (and the author) an easy way out of the dilemma created by her feelings, and it sets up an ending which is cloyingly sentimental and "upbeat."

Too bad, because *The Ritual Bath* could stand up perfectly well without this sort of cheap reassurance at the end. For most of the way it is an impressive piece of work. The Jewishness of its world—the customs, ceremonies, ways of thinking—are beautifully and vividly portrayed, with a nice balance between admiration and irony, sympathy and detachment. And the relation between this insular world and the world outside is sharply portrayed too. Kellerman never glosses over the suspicion and hostility which these strange people arouse in their neighbors. She does not succumb to the current myth that there is no more anti-Semitism in America. She describes anti-Semitism with great power, especially in one shocking scene in which her heroine is harassed by a group of local juvenile delinquents.

Further, the Jewish background, manners, and attitudes of her "detective" are not irrelevant to the murder plot. They fuel that plot, provide the clues, and become integrally connected to the solution. Judaism, as Rena experiences it, is part of the meaning of the murder, just as Catholicism is in the stories of G.K. Chesterton.

Kellerman's second novel about Rina Lazarus, *Sacred and Profane*, just recently published, has been unavailable to me as of this writing (October, 1987).

* * *

In the spectrum of Jewish detectives, the rabbis and others who are officially religious form a fairly narrow band. Most Jewish fictional detectives are as secular, as "unaffiliated," or at best as casual about their adherence to Judaism as most American Jews. In considering them, we find ourselves wondering if they really have to be Jewish at all. Does their Jewishness have anything to do with their character, the way they operate as detectives, or the atmosphere of the novels in which they appear? Or is it simply a thin coating of local color, daubed on the surface?

The answer seems obvious in the case of a large number of fictional Jewish detectives: they have Jewish names, and that is pretty much the only Jewish thing about them. Arthur Lyons' Jacob Asch is a Los Angeles private eye whose adventures are lively and well-written, but his name could be Irish or Italian or impeccably WASP without the need to change a word in the text. The same applies to Shelley Lowenkopf, the New York cop who is sent to Hollywood to solve a murder, in Richard Fliegel's *The Next to Die*; to Mark Schorr's New York cabdriver Simon Jaffe, who fantasizes that he is a private eye out of an old Black Mask serial, in *Red Diamond*,

Private Eye, Ace of Diamonds, and *Diamond Rock*; to Quentin Jacoby, the retired transit cop in J.C.S. Smith's *Jacoby's First Case* and *Nightcap*; to the young homicide detective Max Segal who solves a serial murder in Dan Greenburg's *Love Kills*; to Max Popper, the sleazy literary agent and part-time porn-writer in Michael Wolk's *The Big Picture* (an amusing character whose origins are much closer to Damon Runyon than to the Talmud); to Miles Jacoby, the private eye who moonlights as a prizefighter, in Robert J. Randisi's *Eye in the Ring* and *The Steinway Collection*; to Goldbert (first name never supplied), the ex-football star and retired OSS operative in Arnold Grisman's *Winning Streak.*

This last book illustrates, in an extreme way, the unstated point that all these Jewish-in-name-only detectives seem to be making: American Jews today are so assimilated, so comfortable in the mainstream, that they can move with no strain or self-consciousness in glamourous gentile worlds from which they used to be excluded. They can be police officers, football players, OSS hotshots, tough private eyes—and, as in Grisman's rather absurd fairy tale, several of these things all at once. If Dannay and Lee were writing their novels today, they might call their hero Ellery Cohen—and they wouldn't have to change another word.

A somewhat more ambiguous case of a fictional detective whose Jewishness is all but invisible is Julie Smith's lawyer Rebecca Schwartz. She has a Jewish mother who appears very briefly in *Tourist Trap,* but the real thrust of the character seems to be feminist. What she struggles with throughout the book is the tension between pursuing her dangerous career and getting married, and her Jewish mother seems to be in the story primarily as a device to underline this tension. The question of whether she sees herself as a Jewish woman, with the traditional commitment to husband and family, or as a feminist whose Jewishness is irrelevant could have given some real human depth to Smith's story—especially since the crime in which Rebecca Schwartz becomes involved turns on the conflict between Christian forgiveness and Old Testament ideas of vengeance. But Smith hardly even tries to work this out, and with its most promising implications unrealized, *Tourist Trap* turns out to be a fairly conventional and predictable woman-in-jeopardy suspense story.

* * *

A clutch of recent detective characters are more clearly and unequivocally Jewish; their Jewishness is more closely involved with their personalities and the cases they solve.

Andrew Bergman's Jack LeVine appears for the first time in *The Big Kiss-Off of 1944* (though the book was published in 1974). In many ways he is a chip off the Spade-Marlowe-Archer block. He is tough, stoical, a disillusioned idealist turned cynic; he gets beaten up, is at odds with the official police, frequently talks in wisecracks, and jumps into bed rather casually; and he narrates his own story, in a prose that often has the Chandler ring to it. (Though Chandler would not have been caught dead indulging in Bergman's clumsy habit of elegant variation: unwilling to keep calling his characters by their names, he arbitrarily sticks labels on them. In one scene, for example, in which Thomas E. Dewey appears, Bergman refers to him indiscriminately as "the candidate," "the governor," "the nominee," and "the Republican nominee.")

Jack LeVine is almost Jewish-in-name-only throughout *The Big Kiss-Off*. He does use words like "schmuck" and "putz"; once or twice he is the butt of anti-Semitic cracks from his encounters with crooks and cops: and a brief reference is made to his immigrant parents who are bewildered by the strange unJewish profession he has chosen for himself. But mostly these touches lead nowhere; they are not shown to be a part of LeVine's character, of the way he thinks and the things he does. The exception is one important scene in which a roomful of high-level Army officers and government bigshots try to intimidate LeVine into dropping his client and getting off the case. In LeVine's reaction to this bullying, Bergman gives us a lovely comic picture of Jewish pride and chutzpah; Levine becomes not merely an individualist who dislikes being pushed around, but a distinctly Jewish individualist upholding his honor among the goyim. If LeVine were anything but Jewish, the scene would not be nearly as funny or effective.

In Bergman's second novel, *Hollywood and LeVine*, his hero's Jewishness becomes more important. The action takes place during the era of the Communist witch hunt, shortly after the war, and there is a peculiarly Jewish ambivalence to LeVine's attitude towards both the witch-hunters and the witches. He is never quite caught up in the indiscriminate moral indignation of 1940s liberalism; he displays a skepticism which is reminiscent of the old Talmudic habit of looking at all sides of every question. It becomes clear now that LeVine embodies an older pre-war pragmatism, which is based on real moral values, and which he identifies with New York. Opposed to it is a new post-war sleaziness, which is willing to compromise all values, and this he identifies with Hollywood. The gentile sharks (represented in this novel by Richard Nixon and the FBI) are pouncing on this sleazy new world, and the injustice of their methods enrages LeVine—but at the same time he cannot quite rid himself of an almost Old Testament Prophet feeling that it deserves to be destroyed.

All of this gives life and power to the first two-thirds of *Hollywood and LeVine*, but sadly Bergman does not sustain his vision through the rest of the book. By the end it falls to pieces in almost every conceivable way. Instead of continuing to develop the central theme of the ethical Jew trying to hold onto balance and reason in a corrupt world, he drops it entirely and gives us a sequence of monumental stupidity in which the good guys shoot it out interminably with the bad guys. (*The Big Kiss-Off* also fritters itself away with such a final sequence.) LeVine is joined in this "action-packed climax" by no less than Humphrey Bogart, who as Bergman portrays him is neither an individual character nor a clever spoof of the movie persona; he is simply a stick. And in both novels the detective plot goes flat; the solution to the crime is not the least bit surprising or ingenious, and LeVine gets to it through absolutely no process of reasoning.

The hero of Roger Simon's novels, private detective Moses Wine, is a familiar contemporary, and often Jewish type. He is the 1960s radical who in the 80s has grown a little older, fatter, and balder, and feels guilty because he has settled down in a job and compromised his youthful ideals. Simon does a neat job of characterizing him through the narrational language, and is especially good at suggesting the older generations of radical Jews who form Moses Wine's family inheritance. Wine's elderly Aunt Sonya, the Yiddishkeit and revolutionary who still fights for her principles by trying to radicalize the Jewish old people's center, is a wonderful character; she appears in most of the Wine novels, always in a minor capacity.

Wine's affection for his children, who live with his pretentiously arty divorced wife, also has a distinctly Jewish flavor. Through it Simon shows us the conflict between the Jewish impulse to reform the world and the equally powerful impulse to be a nice respectable bourgeois father.

These themes and social nuances are in the Wine books, but much of the time Simon treats them carelessly and hastily. He never quite works any of them through or integrates them completely with the action. The best of the books is the first, *The Big Fix*, in which Wine is hired by a liberal candidate in a presidential primary to prevent a fanatical old sixties terrorist from sabotaging his campaign by supporting him publicly. The ironies abound, in the contrast that Wine ruefully feels between the old, crazy, undisciplined idealism and the new, genteel, playing-it-safe idealism. But Simon exposes the murderer too soon and allows the last thirty pages of the book to degenerate into conventional private-eye melodramatics.

The second Wine book, *Wild Turkey*, brings the hero into the world of sexual liberation, and hinges on Wine's ambivalent Jewish reaction to it: on the one hand, he believes in total freedom and hates the censors and the bluenoses; on the other hand, his solid bourgeois family instincts are shocked. Simon actually holds onto this theme to the end of the book, and the two parts of Wine's conflict are nicely fused in an effective final image of him dancing and stripping with his kids. But the plot is peremptory, the pivotal character of a Jewish gangster running his empire from a prison cell is weak (we know he is Jewish because he is incapable of speaking a sentence without inserting a Yiddish word into it), and Wine's feats of detection are pretty much non-existent.

In the third of the series, *Peking Duck*, Wine joins a tour to China, and the Jewish, even the individual, elements of his character practically disappear. We get instead a travelogue with bits of international crime thrown into it, and the detective at the center of it could be practically anybody. In *California Roll*, Simon tries to get back on track by having Wine accept a steady highpaying job as security chief for a computer company; his investigation keeps being undermined by the guilt he feels at selling out. The situation is promising, but Simon does very little with it; instead, a lot of conventional private-eye shoot-em-up hokum swamps the book.

Howard Engel's Benny Cooperman is a Canadian private eye who talks, thinks, and acts exactly like every other representative of the species—except that he has a Jewish mother. This juxtaposition seems to be enough for Engel; he feels no obligation to do anything with it, to use Benny's love-exasperation relationship with his mother as a way of getting us deeper into his character or casting light on how he feels about or solves his cases. In every Cooperman book, the action is interrupted from time to time so that Benny can have a conversation with Ma: she nags him, asks him why he can't get a normal steady job like his cousin, and worries that he isn't eating right. All very familiar, but so what? The conversations end, the plot cranks up again, and it is just as if the interludes had never happened.

This odd disjointedness is particularly obvious and annoying in *Murder Sees the Light*, in which Benny's assignment is to locate a Christian fundamentalist preacher who has run out on his church and holed away in the Canadian woods. Benny's relationship with the preacher and his entourage might have inspired Engel to bring out some revealing aspects of his hero's Jewishness, but the opportunity is totally missed.

The plots and characters in the Benny Cooperman books tend to be plodding and predictable—though *The Ransom Game* does have cleverer twists than usual and one neat logical deduction at the end, and *Murder on Location* has an extremely effective portrait of a Jewish gangster, much subtler and more believable than Roger Simon's attempt in *Wild Turkey*. But what spoils the Cooperman books almost beyond redemption is the style.

Engel is in love with stuffing. He fills his pages with longwinded, unevocative, irrelevant details. In *The Suicide Murders*, for instance, it takes him two pages to get his hero across town in his car; he sees two drunks talking on the sidewalk, he reaches into the glove compartment for matches, he drives along the canal and we are given its whole history, each street he passes is named and described. On and on it goes, though absolutely nothing in this interminable narrative adds to our understanding of the character or is used later on in the story. In another section of the same book, Engel's hero begins a chapter with "I won't bore you with the rest of my weekend"—and then fills out the paragraph enumerating the dull events he won't bore us with.

* * *

Jewish cops, despite the example of *Margin for Error*, are far less common than Jewish private eyes, at least in the world of detective fiction. Perhaps this is because Jews so often see themselves as loners; Jewish parents want their sons to take up a profession or go into business for themselves, not work for the government or for a big corporation where they will be dependent on the whims and prejudices of others.

The most successfully realized fictional Jewish cop is Richard Lockridge's Lieutenant Nathan Shapiro of the New York Homicide Squad. Lockridge is best known for the Mr. and Mrs. North books, which he wrote throughout the forties in collaboration with his wife Frances Lockridge. When she died, he stopped writing the North books and turned to several different police-procedural series, of which the Nathan Shapiro books seem to me the best.

In Shapiro Lockridge cleverly manages to unite two paradoxical strains of the American Jewish character: the sense of alienation and the need to belong to a warm and reassuring community. Though Shapiro has a wife (but no children), his need for community is supplied by the police department. His fellow cops are his family; he is able to open his heart to them and kid with them even about such potentially touchy subjects as anti-Semitism.

His sense of alienation comes to Shapiro through his murder cases. Each of them moves him temporarily into a unique and self-contained world, in which he always feels like a fish out of water. Early in each of the Shapiro books, he complains to his captain that he is the wrong man to be on the case; he knows nothing about the world of art, publishing, cafe society, etc.; the people in it make him uncomfortable, he has no clue to their language, social codes, or motivations. By the end of the book, however, it is precisely this sense of alienation which allows him to solve the crime. Because he is an outsider, he can see what the insiders cannot; because he is uneasy, even intimidated, he takes nothing for granted, and no lack of detachment stands in the way of his common sense.

Not many of the Shapiro books are currently available, and I have unfortunately been unable to read them all. Of the five I have read, all share the same weakness. Though everything is real, serious, and honest, the plots lack ingenuity and flair. And so the books stand or fall on the character of Shapiro himself; they seem to work best when Shapiro has a lot to do and say, in a situation and a setting that bring out his funny sympathetic Jewish alienation.

In the best of them, *Preach No More*, Lockridge does what Howard Engel fumbles badly in *Murder Sees the Light*: he brings his Jewish detective in contact with Christian fundamentalism, and strikes some revealing sparks from the confrontation. Sadfaced diffident Shapiro, the son of a rabbi, feels lost in the world of flamboyant evangelical Christianity, and the book has a lot of nice touches that show his bewilderment as he questions the evangelist victim's friends and relations. But ultimately Shapiro solves the case because he is able to see, as his Christian fellow cops cannot, certain universal human feelings that underlie the religious rhetoric of the suspects.

Almost as good is *A Streak of Light*, in which Shapiro investigates the murder of a far-right columnist for a reactionary newspaper. Shapiro has been brought up with the liberal assumptions of any decent Jewish boy, and so this milieu both offends and confuses him. But he does not approach it, and therefore blind himself to it, with selfrighteous indignation. It is full of anti-Semites, but Shapiro has an odd tolerance for them. He sees them as human beings like the rest of us: "we have prejudices even in Brooklyn," he says. And this oddly Jewish willingness to look at every side of the question makes it possible for him to solve the crime.

In *Write Murder Down*, a case that involves the world of New York publishing and the murder of a Southern writer, Shapiro's Jewishness is less important. But his Jewish respect for "the book" does color his attitude towards the venal publishing people involved in the crime. In *The Old Die Young* and *Or Was He Pushed?*, even less is made of Shapiro's Jewishness—and in fact, in both these books Lockridge seems to care less about Shapiro as a character, to spend more time with his partner, the young detective Tony Cook, who is far less interesting.

David Delman's novels about Jacob Horowitz, a police lieutenant in Nassau County, New York, are even harder to find than the Nathan Shapiro books. I have managed to get hold of three of them.

The best of these is *Sudden Death*, which is also the earliest—and, I suspect, the first book in which Horowitz appears. The setting is the world of professional tennis, and the story is narrated by an almost over-the-hill tennis player who is also a suspect in the murder of one of his competitors. This narrator, known only as "Matty," is not a particularly colorful or complex character, and the novel bogs down too often in plodding love scenes between him and his ex-wife; nevertheless, Delman's use of a first-person narrator allows him to pull off a stunning *tour de force* with his detective hero. Horowitz is never seen except through Matty's eyes; we are never permitted to enter his point of view or listen in on his thoughts. And the way Matty sees him is as a kind of Old Testament God.

There is nothing solemn or pretentious about this. Delman never suggests that Horowitz is *really* a supernatural presence; nor does he ever treat him as a Symbol rather than a human being. The implication that Horowitz can be equated with God is ironic, and Delman uses it to make a point. Through Horowitz's impact on the "I" of the story—and therefore on the reader—Delman plays on a feeling all of us have about Authority. It is a feeling that reveals itself in big ways (our sense of helplessness in times of disappointment or grief) and in small ways (our uneasiness when we notice a police car driving next to us on the street).

This note is struck in the narrator's very first description of Horowitz:

> a huge man ... ugly in a way ... with such force ... as if he had always been bigger than everybody and had had to master techniques for avoiding unnecessary

destruction ... nothing gentle about his eyes ... while his lips curved in smiles, his eyes watched voraciously, as if in a state of near starvation for the lies you would eventually set before him.

Like the God of *Genesis*, Horowitz seems to see everything that goes on inside people, yet he is constantly playing ignorant, asking questions whose answers he knows already, testing. ("Where is Abel thy brother?" God asks Cain, the first murderer, early in *Genesis*.) It is as if he wants his people to exercise free will, to tell the truth without intimidation, to be good without coercion—or to fall into the abyss when they fail the test. Thus the following conversation, full of overtones, between Horowitz and Matty:

'The truth saves time, my wise old grandfather used to say. Most of my people find that out sooner or later.'

'Your people?'

'The people I deal with when I work on a case. I take a proprietary interest in them.'

Also like the God of the Old Testament, Horowitz is unpredictable; you never know how to take him or what he is likely to do next. Sometimes he is indulgent and lets a suspect disagree with him, even argue with him (as God allowed Abraham to argue with him about the fate of the people of Sodom). But this indulgence can end as abruptly as it began: "So don't get too smart with me," Horowitz says to Matty. "A little pertness, that I don't mind. But don't push too hard. When irritated, this Jew pushes back."

The unpredictability comes through with neat

underplayed irony in the way Delman handles Horowitz's entrances and exits throughout the story. He never comes into a room after announcing himself; he is always suddenly there, when the characters least expect him, often when they are in the middle of intimate conversations they would prefer to conceal from him. And he leaves rooms just as suddenly and arbitrarily.

This sense of Horowitz as a mysterious, quasi-supernational force is never far from the way the other characters in the novel think and talk about him. "The man's a devil," somebody says of him. And Horowitz cheerfully agrees: "I'm a demon." At another point he is described as "pure hunter"—that is, the fateful hunter-god from whom there is no escape, whose arrow finds our heart no matter how far we run. Two things Matty says about him reinforce these feelings: "When Horowitz moves, the rest of us become irrelevant," And, "He moves in mysterious ways."

The image of Horowitz as Old Testament God is worked out carefully and consistently throughout the novel. The world of tennis is presented as an appropriate arena for such a God to operate in: it is a world in which skill, experience, and strength are absolutely essential, yet always at the mercy of arbitrary fate, always subject to the sudden crazy bounce of a ball. Tennis is Delman's metaphor for an uncertain world in which God is an enigma, and the ending of the novel, the solution to the murder, carries through with this same idea. At the end God—Horowitz—shows arbitrary mercy to the killer; he saves him from the executioner but reserves an even more horrible fate for him. And in the last, extremely witty touch in the novel, Horowitz lets the world know about his final ironic twist of mercy not by appearing in person but by delivering his message out of the blue, from on high—in the form of a telegram, the closest twentieth-century equivalent to an angelic messenger.

Along with Delman's playful metaphysics, *Sudden Death*, also holds up well as a detective story. The clues are ingenious and plausible, and Horowitz uses them with impeccable logic—as God, after all, ought to do. After finishing this highly enjoyable variation on the Jewish cop, I looked forward eagerly to more Horowitz books.

With immense disappointment I discovered, in the two books I was able to read—*He Who Digs a Grave* and *Murder in the Family*—that *Sudden Death* appears to be a onetime fluke. *He Who Digs a Grave* was published only a year later, and already Delman has jettisoned everything about Horowitz that makes him an original and entertaining character. The story is no longer told in the first person by one of the characters in it; instead Delman makes the fatal error of introducing us into Horowitz's point of view. What we find going on in his mind—in this book and in *Murder in the Family*, which was written ten years later—are purely conventional thoughts and reactions. He is no longer God. His mystery is gone; so is his arbitrariness. But unfortunately he has not been replaced by an individual interesting human being.

In *He Who Digs a Grave* Horowitz takes on a case in a small southwestern town, in *Murder in the Family* he becomes embroiled in international intrigue in Portugal, but neither setting is re-created with much sharpness or color. And in both books Delman gets Horowitz involved in a love affair, as dreary and predictable as the subsidiary love affair that was the only blot on *Sudden Death*. The murder plot in *He Who Digs a Grave* is ingenious and satisfyingly worked out at the end; in *Murder in the Family* even that ingenuity has failed. But none of this matters very much, for the real trouble with the later Horowitz books is that God is dead.

* * *

Many Jews, especially since the end of World War II, have been college professors, and so it is not surprising that a Jewish professor-detective has made his appearance. He is Henry Spearman, and he appears in two novels by Marshall Jevons, *Murder at the Margin* and *The Fatal Equilibrium*. Spearman, a professor of economics and a German-Jewish refugee, seems to be partly inspired by Milton Friedman, but that is about as far as his Jewishness goes, at least overtly.

Yet he cannot be relegated entirely to the Jewish-in-name-only category. There is something about Spearman's pragmatic-idealistic attitude towards life which makes him, even without identification tags, a recognizable and witty portrait of a certain type of Jewish academician. He may not <u>have</u> to be Jewish, but people like Spearman often are—and are often refugees from European persecution too. And though some stiffness, even pedantry, occasionally seeps into Jevons' prose, these novels are amusing, instructive, and in the unraveling of their puzzles absolutely fair; they show that principles of economics are not so far from Talmudic logic.

Jews have been less prominent in the world of baseball than in academia, and this may be why R.D. Rosen, in *Strike Three, You're Dead*, chose to create Harvey Blissberg, a Jewish detective who is also a center fielder for a major league team. Harvey as a ballplayer and Harvey as a Jew relate in several ways which allow Rosen to say a lot about both minority groups. For example, he shows us what Harvey's baseball success means to his fellow Jews. It is an impeccable guarantee of Americanization, a constant reassurance that anti-Semitism can be overcome and

Jews can be part of America without ceasing to be Jewish. At the same time, it is a peculiar thing for a Jew to be doing, and the novel suggests this through the attitudes of Harvey's family: pride whenever he has a good day at bat, but always the unspoken question, "What kind of a job is this for a nice Jewish boy?"

Harvey's own ambivalence toward baseball becomes an integral part of the story. Baseball is the passion of his life, but at he same time he can never quite overcome his feeling that it is trivial, "only a game." After all, Jews are supposed to do something serious, valuable, socially responsible in the world. To some extent Harvey's urge to investigate his teammate's murder is connected to this belief.

But the two aspects of Rosen's hero—Harvey the ballplayer and Harvey the Jew—never come together quite comfortably in the novel. They always seem to be at war with each other, and for a while the author seems uncertain which he cares about the most. He resolves this conflict by the end, however. The baseball element pushes the Jewish element to the background; the solution to the crime hinges on a curious and ingenious motive which makes sense only in the world of baseball but has nothing whatever to do with the hero's Jewishness. And the last forty pages of the book, after we know the solution, are taken up with action sequences that exploit the geography of a ball park but leave the pleasures of logical deduction totally forgotten.

Rosen's second novel, *Fadeaway*, confirms the outcome of the war. Harvey Blissberg has retired from baseball and become a private eye specializing in cases from the world of sports. (*Fadeaway* deals with basketball.) But Harvey is no longer Jewish; at least, this fact about him isn't even alluded to in the course of the book. He appears to have ended up in the limbo of detectives who are Jewish in name only.

Another Jewish detective who comes to the world of crime from an unexpected direction is the hero of Cornelius Hirschberg's *Florentine Finish*. (This novel is a curiosity in many ways. Hirschberg was a retired businessman who wrote *Florentine Finish* when he was in his sixties. Appearing in 1963, it was his first work of fiction and, as far as I have been able to tell, his last.) Saul Handy, an ex-cop, works as a salesman in the famous New York City block, from Fifth to Sixth Avenue on Forty-Sixth Street, where most of America's jewelry trade—diamond-cutting, designing, wholesaling, and wheeling-and-dealing—goes on. It is a largely (though not exclusively) Jewish world, populated by all kinds of Jews, from Hassidim to hustlers, from artists to junk-peddlers. One of the great merits of this novel is the verve, the humor, and the wealth of fascinating detail with which Hirschberg portrays this world. It has probably never been brought alive more vividly, in or outside of the detective-story form.

Hirschberg's hero, Saul Handy, is the perfect detective for this world. He is both in it and apart from it: in it because he earns his precarious livelihood by hustling gems; apart from it because he joined it late in his life and started off as a policeman in a different city. This dualism creates, throughout *Florentine Finish*, a subplot that accompanies the murder plot. Saul is concerned not only with the question of the killer's identity but with the question of whether he himself is or is not committed to this eccentric Jewish world in which he works. At the end of the novel he answers both questions at once: the revelation of the killer's identity fuses perfectly with Saul's decision about his future.

Florentine Finish illustrates delightfully one of the great potential strengths of the Jewish detective story. It shows that a completely logical, well worked-out exercise in puzzle-solving can take place in an atmosphere that is lively and colorful, down-to-earth, warm, humanly messy. Satisfying displays of deduction need not be limited, as Auden thought, to the genteel villages or aristocratic oakpaneled studies of the "classic" Anglo-American detective story.

* * *

But this liveliness has its potential dangers, all of which are illustrated by four more Jewish detectives: George Baxt's Sylvia Plotkin, a high school teacher who later becomes a best-selling author; Herbert Resnicow's Alexander Gold, a consulting engineer; Marvin Kaye's Marty Gold, a druggist; and Silky Pincus, the private eye hero of Leo Rosten's only venture into the genre, *Silky!*. I lump all these together because the books in which they appear belong to the most dismal, if not downright repellent category of Jewish detective story: they all aim at being comic.

It is true, of course, that some of the best Jewish detectives are comic: Rabbi David Small, for example, or Lieutenant Nathan Shapiro. But the comedy of these characters is grounded in their human, believable foibles; they are real people, with many dimensions to them, a few of which happen to make us laugh. They are comic in the same sense as Sherlock Holmes, Hercule Poirot, and Nick Charles. It might be argued, in fact, that the detective-story form is itself comic; it deals with death, guilt, and evil, the same ingredients that tragedy deals with, but in a way that distances us from their grim reality and usually leads to a happy ending.

But the comedy of Baxt, Resnicow, Kaye, and Rosten is not rooted in sharp human observation at all. It is rooted rather in the underlying assumption that Jewishness is somehow funny in and of itself. Merely mentioning that a detective character is Jewish and giving him or her certain comic-strip Jewish traits is automatically grounds for hilarity. The intention of these authors, in other words, is to make their readers feel superior to their characters. And so their books produce neither hearty bellylaughs nor gentle chuckles, but sniggers.

Silky! is the saddest case, because it comes from the same writer who years ago gave us *The Education of Hyman Kaplan*. In the Kaplan stories, the hero's Yiddishisms, inaccurate English, and grotesque accent were at the service of a human insight; Rosten wanted to show us the gap between the immigrant's ineptitude with American manners and language and his desperate need to become an American. We feel affection, in fact admiration, for Kaplan because we recognize the human roots of his absurdity.

In *Silky!*, Rosten's Jewish private eye is absurd merely because he is Jewish and has the temerity to be a private eye. To reinforce this joke, the novel's one and only joke, Rosten cannot let him open his mouth without bringing out a Yiddish word or a "funny" locution. It is all so overblown that eventually, and inevitably it becomes intolerable, like the conversation of someone who can speak only in puns.

George Baxt's Sylvia Plotkin, who makes her first appearance in *A Parade of Cockeyed Creatures* and subsequently in *Satan Is a Woman* and *"I," Said the Demon*, begins reasonably well as a wry, independent, witty woman. But Baxt loses control of her quickly, and turns her into a coy, husband-hunting old-maid stereotype, salivating over a handsome police officer—who of course does all the thinking about the crime. The idea of a Jewish spinster lusting after a Nordic cop seems so titillatingly droll to Baxt that he destroys his character for the sake of it. Besides being degrading to women in general and Jewish women in particular, these novels are not even very good as detective stories. The endings are arbitrary; nobody *solves* anything; we are simply told, after a couple of hundred pages, who did it.

Herbert Resnicow has produced three books about Alexander Gold, engineering consultant and genius, all narrated by his wife Norma. I have read *The Gold Solution* and *The Gold Deadline*; I have been unable to locate any copies of *The Gold Frame*.

The publisher's blurbs compare the Golds to Nick and Nora Charles, an egregious example of false advertising even in an era that thrives on it. There is nothing about what the Golds say that can conceivably be called witty. They either go in for insufferable cuteness, or they scream unforgivable insults at each other and at everybody else. The gratuitous nastiness of what passes for repartee between them makes them among the most repulsive characters in detective literature—it is a mystery why the other people in the book do not kick them in the teeth—yet Resnicow obviously does not <u>mean</u> them to strike us that way. He wants us to be charmed by their cruelty, insensitivity, and bad manners—apparently his view of what is charming and characteristic about Jews.

The plots of the Gold books are locked-room puzzles, and they make one appreciate John Dickson Carr, in spite of his snobbishness and lush overwriting. In both Gold books that I have read, the solution to the locked-room puzzle stares us in the face from the start—but nobody thinks of it, nobody asks about it, until at the very end Alexander Gold suddenly pops out with it, and everybody says what a genius he is.

Marvin Kaye's two novels about Marty Gold, *My Son, the Druggist* and *My Brother, the Druggist*, almost fail to qualify as detective stories. They are mostly comic-suspense capers, with an element or two of mystery thrown in. Once again Kaye's hero has no character, no point of view, nothing in him that tell us about human nature or Jewish human nature. He simply "talks Jewish," and we are invited to laugh at the delicious incongruity between such talk and the conventional adventures he goes through. If you find this sort of thing funny, you must join the French in worshipping Jerry Lewis movies.

* * *

All the authors I have discussed so far are American. The detective story is still alive and well in its traditional European homes—England, France, the Netherlands, and the Scandinavian countries. Yet it has been very difficult for me to discover Jewish detective characters coming out of these countries. Partly, no doubt, this is because Europe has a much smaller Jewish population than the United States. But the chief reason, I suspect, is that despite gigantic changes since World War II, Jews still feel less at home in Europe than they do here.

Still, there is one extraordinary practitioner of the Jewish detective story in England. Her name is S.T. Haymon, and her three novels featuring the Norwich policeman Detective Inspector Benjamin Jurnet ought to be a lot better known than they are.

In one respect they are different from any other detective stories I have discussed. They are concerned, deeply and fundamentally, with spiritual, even mystical issues. Haymon treats Judaism as a religion, not merely a social phenomenon, and she builds her action around the relationships between Judaism's religious vision and that of Christianity. Not that the books have no social observation in them: they deal prominently, for example, with the position of the Jew in a society that has a long tradition of anti-Semitism and state ecclesiasticism. But ultimately the social portraiture in Haymon's books serves mainly as a realistic context for stories that cut much deeper.

The murder in her first book, *Death and the Pregnant Virgin*, is set in a saintly shrine which has aroused the fanatical piety of people in a small isolated English town. The contrast between the adoring crowds who have come to pay homage to, and be cured by, the saint's statue, and the TV cameras that are covering the spectacle, is basic to the book, which plays throughout with the paradox of faith in a modern secular technological world. The theme is deepened by the discovery, confirmed by the most rigorous medical examination, that the dead girl is pregnant but also unquestionably a virgin.

The solution to this metaphysical puzzle is worked out with all the logic and fairness of the best "Golden Age" detective stories; the clues are given to us, and Inspector Jurnet eventually interprets them with brilliant acumen. But more important, the solution takes us even more deeply into the spiritual dilemmas that are central themes of the book. At the end, we not only find out who the murderer is, but we confront the question that separates Christianity from Judaism, whether the Messiah has come or is yet to come.

Jurnet himself, deeply troubled by an ambivalent sense of identity, is the perfect observer, and battleground, for the novel's spiritual concerns. He is in love with a Jewish woman who insists she will not marry him unless he converts to Judaism. Jurnet is a casual agnostic who has given very little thought to religious questions before. He is not Jewish—yet in the course of the book certain circumstances make him wonder if his ancestors might have been Jewish after all. He is Jew and Christian and agnostic all at once, and this confusion within him colors his approach to the murder.

His investigation of this murder becomes intertwined with his investigation of his own past, the conflict within his soul. His growing awareness of something Jewish in him reaches its climax in the solution to the murder. That solution emerges <u>because</u> of Jurnet's spiritual crisis, and in turn it brings about Jurnet's next step towards resolving that crisis.

The writing in *Death and the Pregnant Virgin* is beautiful and evocative, without ever being fancy or pretentious. The characters—not only Jurnet but everyone else from the townspeople to his fellow policemen—are solid and real, and always more complex than they seem at first. And just as complex is Haymon's recreation of the brooding atmosphere of rural England. Her Norwich town is never the simple stereotype of the sleepy little hamlet (with evil lurking beneath) that so many Agatha Christie imitators have dished up from across the Atlantic.

The second Haymon novel, *Ritual Murder*, more than fulfills the promise of the first. At the center of the story is the death of a choirboy under circumstances that recall the medieval ritual murders of which Jews were often accused. Medieval England is palpably present throughout the novel, though Haymon never goes in for historical flashbacks; she simply makes us feel the ancient impulses in the behavior of present day people. And the solution to the crime—particularly ingenious and well-grounded in logic—implies some disturbing ideas about the connection between evil and innocence, ignorance and cruelty, piety and anti-Semitism.

Jurnet has grown in complexity since the first novel too. He is now studying for his conversion to Judaism, which gives Haymon the opportunity to produce some trenchant portraits of today's English-Jewish community. But Jurnet's ambivalence, his alienation from both the Christian and Jewish worlds,

Is This Any Job for a Nice Jewish Boy? 53

comes through even more strongly now. Haymon shows us how this ambivalence connects with Jurnet's job as a policeman, how his constant contact with the extremes of human evil keeps him from believing in God while filling him with the urgent desire to believe in God. Judaism is central to *Ritual Murder*, and so is Christianity, but both are used as springboards to the deeper theme: the mystery of faith in an evil world.

In the most recent Haymon novel, *Stately Homicide*, Jurnet investigates a murder in an old countryhouse with an ominous Elizabethan history. Once again historical events are intertwined with the details of a modern crime, and both cast a light on Jurnet's personal situation.

In *Stately Homicide*, however, Jurnet's ambiguous Jewishness is less important than in the two earlier books. He is still with his Jewish fiancée, still studying for his conversion to Judaism, and still finding it difficult to pretend that he is motivated by love of the One God rather than love of the girl. But this time around the human implications of this struggle interest Haymon more than the religious implications, and in fact the underlying theme of the book is love—its irrational and compulsive nature, the strange variety of ways in which human beings can express it to one another.

Though the plot is clever and intricate, and Haymon's writing and characterization are up to her highest standard, the emotional pressure of *Stately Homicide* is somehow lower than usual. I think this is because she has put Jurnet's spiritual conflict on hold most of the way. No doubt she will return to it in more depth and detail in subsequent Jurnet books, all of which I look forward to with pleasure.

* * *

So the Jewish detective story has been freed from bondage since the end of World War II, and some genuine heights have been reached. Nevertheless, I cannot avoid the feeling that its potentialities have not yet been fully explored. The Catholic detective story may have reached its peak in Chesterton's Father Brown stories, the hard-boiled private-eye genre in the works of Hammett, Chandler, and Ross MacDonald. But the Jewish detective story, though from one point of view it is thousands of years old, is actually quite young, a post-war phenomenon. Its greatest achievements may still be waiting in the wings.

It is impossible to predict what forms those achievements will take. But I have no doubt the Jewish detective story will continue to flourish. After all, God was the first detective, and He made us in His own image.

* * *

EDITOR'S NOTE: The one major writer of Jewish detective fiction not discussed in the foregoing essay is James Yaffe himself, who debuted in *Ellery Queen's Mystery Magazine* in 1943 at the age of fifteen with the first of six stories about Paul Dawn of the NYPD's Department of Impossible Crimes, clever formal puzzles influenced by Queen and John Dickson Carr and written with precocious gusto. Dawn was an ethnically neutral character, but after the war, Yaffe went on to become a noted mainstream novelist and playwright on subjects of American Jewish life. Supporting his own idea of the post-war acceptability of Jewish themes in mystery fiction, he began in 1952 a series of short stories about a Jewish mother who solves her New York policeman son's cases for him in armchair-detective style. In these stories, Yaffe combined the fair-play plotting of the Dawn stories with greater sophistication in style and character. The character known only as Mom had appeared in eight stories by

1968, but not until *A Nice Murder for Mom* (1988) did she have a book length appearance, now relocated in Mesa Grande, Colorado, where her widowed son Dave is working as investigator for the public defender. The first Mom book is a good formal detective novel, but the second, *Mom Meets Her Maker* (1990), is better still, probably Yaffe's finest achievement in the detective-story form. Not only does it have a dazzling elaborate and generously clued puzzle plot worthy of the Ellery Queen team, but also a fine depiction of the ambivalent attitudes of Jews toward that most Christian (and most commercialized) of national holidays, Christmas. It is hoped that the continuing series of Mom novels will lead to the short stories being collected in book form.

Several of the authors discussed in Yaffe's essay have published additional novels since it was written. Faye Kellerman wrote an impressive historical mystery about Jewish conversos in Elizabethan England in *The Quality of Mercy* (1989), while her series sleuth Rina Lazarus appears for a third case in *Milk and Honey* (1990). (Her husband Jonathan Kellerman, whose novels about child psychologist Alex Delaware generally lack specific Jewish content, wrote a bestseller about an Israeli policeman hunting a serial killer in 1988's *The Butcher's Theater*.) Joseph Telushkin's Rabbi Daniel Winter solves a second case in *The Final Analysis of Dr. Stark* (1988). S.T. Haymon's series about Ben Jurnet has continued with *Death of a God* (1987) and *A Very Particular Murder* (1989). Roger L. Simon's Moses Wine returns in *The Straight Man* (1986) and *Raising the Dead* (1988), the latter involving a visit to Israel.

PROTESTANT MYSTERIES

by Jon L. Breen

For many years, it seemed that Protestant clergy just weren't cut out to be popular fictional sleuths. The most famous detecting cleric, G.K. Chesterton's Father Brown, was of course a Roman Catholic, and most of those who followed him through the fifties and into the sixties were of the same faith. When Harry Kemelman introduced Rabbi David Small in the sixties, he established the second most famous clergy sleuth in fiction and added to the puzzle of why there were so few Protestants.

Protestant clergy detectives were not entirely unknown, however. An early example turned up in an unlikely venue for the religious detective story: *Black Mask* magazine. The Reverend McGregor Daunt, created by J. Paul Suter, first appeared in "The Problem of the Man Who Sowed the Wind" (November 1924). A Cleveland preacher of unspecified denomination, Daunt has a unique advantage among clergy detectives: he is a millionaire, who is able to keep a "palatial" hunting lodge (for thinking rather than hunting) twenty miles from his city church and to employ a manservant and a French chef. He seldom preaches, hiring others to do it for him.

Daunt, who had already mastered law and medicine before turning to divinity, does not let his profession inconvenience him in his amateur detective endeavors, and he belongs more to the Transcendent Detective school of Sherlock Holmes and his imitators than to the tough-guy school associated with *Black Mask* or to the more down-to-earth and realistic mode of clergy detectives to follow. He is self-described as a "bachelor, and known as something of a woman-hater." His first case is an extremely unlikely pseudoscientific one drawing on the twenties Egyptology fad. Daunt quotes a moral lesson from the Apocrypha at the end ("By whatsoever things a man sins, by these he is punished"), but there is little theological content to the story.

A later and better Daunt tale is "The Foot-Washing Baptist" (August 1926), in which the backwoodsy Tennessee preacher of the title tells Daunt he has come to Cleveland to bring down the ungodly psychic/conjurer known as the Great Malvolio. The plot is scarcely more likely than that of the earlier case, but the general storytelling has improved and Daunt's solution is based on his ability to judge the genuineness of another Man of God. Daunt is no sleuthing immortal, but he seems to have the distinction (unless you include Melville Davisson Post's very religious layman Uncle Abner) of being the first Protestant clergy sleuth.

Aside from this short-story character, whose cases were never collected, there have been a few scattered examples of the Protestant religious detective. William David Spencer provides a good overview of them in his *Mysterium and Mystery*. The earliest identified is Vicar Westerham, the one-shot sleuth of Victor L. Whitechurch's *The Crime at Diana's Pool* (1972). Spencer believes Westerham could have turned into a memorable clergy sleuth had Whitechurch stuck with him, but the vicar "fell out of step and was left behind in the march of that vast host of competent, tight-lipped professionals who staffed the remainder of Whitechurch's mysteries" (page 205).

Spencer's comments suggest why none of these subsequent clergy sleuths achieved the status of Father Brown or Rabbi Small: C.A. Alington's Archdeacons

Craggs and Castleton ("...when the chips are down, Alington's archdeacons are a secular lot, indistinguishable from the nonecclesiastics around them," page 209), who appeared in four mysteries beginning with *Archdeacons Afloat* (1946); Margaret Scherf's Reverend Martin Buell ("As the far extreme of the untheological, unamiable clerical sleuth, Buell is a sheer delight in his perversity," page 214), who solved seven mysteries beginning with *Always Murder a Friend* (1948); Stephen Chance's (Philip Turner's) Reverend Septimus Treloar ("He lies blithely when he feels the need to do so," page 230), a former policeman who appears in four books beginning with *Septimus and the Danedyke Mystery* (1973); Barbara Ninde Byfield's Father Simon Bede ("one of the least theologically integrated and realistic of the clerical sleuths," page 240), who debuted in *Solemn High Murder* (1975), written with Frank L. Tedeschi, and appeared in decreasing roles in three subsequent novels by Byfield solo; and Isabelle Holland's Reverend Claire Aldington ("a rather catty, unpleasant person who has a strong conflict in her perspective," page 248), who appeared first in *A Death at St. Anselm's* (1984) and most recently in *A Fatal Advent* (1989). (The latter is a good detective novel that makes effective use of its New York Episcopal church background, but it lacks the fascinating theological tangents of the best religious mysteries.)

All of the above are Anglicans and thus close theologically to the Roman Catholics who for whatever reason have comprised most of the clergy sleuths. Spencer also discusses Matthew Head's (John Canaday's) missionary Dr. Mary Finney (he questions the "authenticity of her calling," page 255), who appeared in *The Cabinda Affair* (1949) and three later books; and James L. Johnson's clerical espionage agent Sebastian ("starkly ascetic and charged with a nearly overwhelming preoccupation with God," page 287), who appeared in *Code Name Sebastian* (1967) and five subsequent adventures. In his *Bedside Companion to Crime* (1989), H.R.F. Keating cites an ecclesiastical sleuth not discussed in detail by Spencer: Archdeacon Toft, presumably another Anglican, who appeared in several novels by Thurman Warriner, beginning with *Method in his Murder* (1950). Keating admits, though, that Toft is not necessarily the principal sleuth; most sources list the private detective Mr. Scotter in that role in the books in which Toft appears, and Spencer consigns him to the role of "saintly sidekick" rather than "clerical sleuth."

The present essay will concentrate on two authors: Charles Merrill Smith, also discussed by Spencer, who has come the closest to creating a popular Protestant clerical sleuth to stand with Father Brown and Rabbi Small, and Gaylord Larsen, who does not write of clergy detectives and is not covered by Spencer but is representative of those evangelical Christian writers who use the detective story as a vehicle for witness.

Methodist clergyman Smith was already a well-known author of non-fiction when he turned to detective novels. He made his debut with a 1965 bestseller, *How to Become a Bishop Without Being Religious*, and followed it up with satirical volumes like *When the Saints Go Marching Out* (1969) and *The Pearly Gates Syndicate; or How to Sell Real Estate in Heaven* (1971). As often becomes clear in the series he wrote about the Reverend C.P. Randollph, Smith's greatest talent was as an informal essayist rather than a fiction writer, but at his best he was capable of a good detective story and at his least was never less than entertaining and provocative.

Reverend Randollph and the Wages of Sin (1974) begins with trendy associate pastor Dan Gantry meeting his new boss at the Chicago airport. By the third page, Randollph, Gantry, and the bishop known only as

Protestant Mysteries

Freddie are drinking in the airport bar. (It is pointed out immediately that "Reverend" is not really a title, but that the battle on that matter of usage has long been lost—hence the use of it as a title in all the books in the series.)

The Reverend Cesare Paul "Con" Randollph, former Los Angeles Rams quarterback, now a church historian on sabbatical from his academic post, is cast much more against type than his best-known Catholic and Jewish sleuthing colleagues. The first statement made about him is the bishop's: "He should be one of the first off....I've never known C.P. to travel other than first class—at least not when someone else is paying the bill" (page 9, Avon 1982 paperback edition). From his first appearance, Randollph is pegged as a snappy dresser, wearing a "nifty, blue houndstooth Norfolk jacket over a navy turtleneck..." (page 9).

Randollph is in Chicago to serve as interim pastor of the Church of the Good Shepherd. The trustees, who had supported the forcibly retired outgoing pastor, had money-man O.B. Smelser picked out as the successor, but the bishop, concerned about dropping contributions to charitable causes and suspecting irregularities in the church's finances, has brought in Randollph, who has never before pastored a church.

The new pastor's church is as unconventional as he is. The Church of the Good Shepherd, forty stories high with a gothic tower on top, is a commercial building as well as a place of worship. The pastor has a penthouse apartment under the tower, and is able to live a life of luxury not all that far removed (come to think of it) from the millionaire preacher McGregor Daunt. The wealthy church has a small membership, most of whom seldom attend; the bulk of its worshippers are tourists and conventioneers.

In the third chapter, TV journalist Samantha Stack comes to interview Randollph. Sam is a thirtyish beauty, divorced, a declared atheist who immediately asks Con about his sex life and invites him to appear on her TV show. The series will feature many encounters on Sam's show, giving Smith a chance to go into his essayist mode to comment on present-day religious and social issues. The opponent this time is an anti-porn, anticommunist crusader, the Reverend Jeff Davis Troutman of the Christ Against Communism Foundation. Surprised to be asked by Sam if he is a religious man, Randollph replies, "If you mean by that do I spend long hours in devotional activities or do I hold conventional pious attitudes, then no, I'm not a religious man" (page 78). We learn that Randollph was once on the evangelical staff of the Association of Athletes for Christ but left that organization at the same time he left football "because they both seemed unreal" (page 79).

Of the major clergy sleuths, Randollph is surely the most irreverent. Reading the funeral service of the novel's murder victim (the strangled wife of a church board member), he reflects inwardly that a passage from Corinthians is "sublimely phrased nonsense" and "lilting dualistic goop" (page 110). This clearly is not a preacher who finds all scripture infallible. As the story goes on Randollph reacts strongly to the homophobia of the series' obligatory continuing cop Lieutenant Michael Casey and reveals himself surprisingly tolerant of extra-marital sex.

In this first novel and in subsequent ones, Bishop Freddie is the best secondary character, always offering his pragmatic advice to Randollph, as the new pastor finds his way in the business of running a church. This time, Freddie's disquisition on the limits of pastoral counseling is especially enjoyable. Church secretary Miss Windfall is another figure who will recur; she is determined to keep Randollph's nose to the grindstone, and their relationship is very much like that of John Putnam Thatcher and Miss Corsa in Emma Lathen's Wall Street mystery series. (Indeed, Smith is probably closer in style to the Lathen team than to any other writer in the mystery field.)

The well-drawn killer's identity in *Wages of Sin* comes as a genuine surprise, and the book's theme—that distortion of Biblical teachings can result in madness and murder—is effectively demonstrated. The puzzle is much more soundly constructed as well as being better integrated with the essay-writing than in the later novels. All the Randollph books have their attractions, but the first is very much the best detective story.

The novel finishes with the suggestion of coming sex between Con and Sam. Smith will have fun with the will-they-or-won't-they and did-they-or-didn't-they question until marriage finally intervenes.

The second book, *Reverend Randollph and the Avenging Angel* (1977), begins with Randollph back on Sam's TV show, arguing Biblical inerrancy with another fundamentalist. Clarence Higbee, a Bunterish-Jeevesian servant, has been added to the regular cast as Randollph's gourmet cook. Con is still an interim pastor and is finding the job mostly administrative.

The plot centers around the impending wedding of one of Sam's sorority sisters, movie star Lisa Julian. Con is to preside, and Freddie fills him in on some of the pitfalls of a formal church wedding. Lisa is murdered by a poker-wielding blond intruder. The solution proves fairly guessable, and the book points up a continuing problem with the Randollph series: while the continuing characters come to life for the reader, the suspects and other one-shot figures usually do not.

Exactly what denomination does Randollph belong

to? Some sources have claimed Episcopal, but one scene with Higbee (an Anglican to the bone) makes it clear that is not Con's church. The denomination is never specified, but the presence of a bishop makes me think that Randollph (like his creator) is probably a Methodist.

In *Avenging Angel*, there is certainly a strong implication Con is sleeping with Sam, but it isn't spelled out. At the end of the book, he proposes, but Sam tearfully refuses. Though she now describes herself as an agnostic rather than an atheist, she does not see herself as a suitable pastor's wife and is reluctant to give up her own career. As the third book, *Reverend Randollph and the Fall from Grace, Inc.* (1978), begins, Sam is still refusing.

Each book has provided a representative of the legalistic fundamentalist clergy for mainliner Con to skewer. This time he's been appointed to a committee to look at the credentials of TV evangelist Prince Hartman, a potential Democratic (??) candidate for the Senate who is seeking recognition in Con's denomination. Providing the requisite murder victim, Hartman's gluttonous aide Charlie Klemm is poisoned by chocolates seemingly intended for his boss.

In this book, black divinity student Elijah Roundtree is chosen as a trainee pastor and Randollph does his reverse discrimination number, a reactionary note that seems out of step with the liberal spirit of the other books. Con appears on TV again, confronting Roundtree on Sam's news spot. As the cards are stacked, of course, Randollph is perfectly right: the unpleasant Roundtree is arrogantly trading on his ethnicity to try to guarantee himself a position he would not otherwise deserve. The question is why Smith chose to stack them that way.

The plot of *Fall from Grace* is much thinner than

in the first two books: the main misdirection is so heavy-handed most readers will see through it a hundred pages before Randollph does. Aside from Randollph, Bishop Freddie, and cop Casey, the characters are oversimplified and cartoonish.

The end of the book raises a possibility, of Con becoming the permanent pastor, that is realized in the fourth book, *Reverend Randollph and the Holy Terror* (1980), concerning a serial killer who sends clergy poetry before bumping them off. This is also the book in which Con and Sam are married. Their bedroom scene is more explicit than anything earlier in the series, and certainly Smith <u>implies</u> this is the first time for Con and Sam. He still doesn't close the door completely, though, on the reader who chooses to believe otherwise about their pre-marital relationship. One almost has the feeling Smith intended the couple to have pre-marital sex but drew back at the last minute, part of the softening and conventionalizing process that often happens to series characters as they become more popular.

In *Holy Terror*, the series continues to deteriorate as detective fiction. There is little violence and little real detection. The major events run to meals, church committee meetings, and talkshow appearances—Con again confronts an anti-porn crusader in extended debate on Sam's TV show. Smith's characters bounce back so readily, are so quick with a quip in times of crisis, that the terrors of the novel seem quite unreal.

But the fifth book, *Reverend Randollph and the Unholy Bible* (1983), is a good deal better, not only offering more action and detective work but a more interesting religious message as well. On the very first page, Randollph himself discovers the body: 85-year-old Johannes Humbrecht, a former Northwestern history professor turned reclusive junk-collector, found brutally bludgeoned to death by a baseball bat in his "rotting old mansion." Randollph tells Casey Humbrecht was his "token poor parishioner" (page 11).

Randollph is taken for a ride to see a Chicago gangster who believes Con killed Humbrecht for a unique treasure: an unknown 48th copy of the Gutenberg Bible. The gangster wants to will the Bible to the Pope and thus receive remission of his many sins. Smith chose a good McGuffin here—the story is studded with interesting historical tidbits about Gutenberg and his product.

In an unusual infusion of physical action, Randollph uses his football prowess to escape the villain's minions and later feels guilty for enjoying his feeling of power over the crooks. Foreign travel also figures in the story, as Randollph travels to Rome for an audience with the first American Pope, John XXIV.

Another of the elements that make this novel unusual (and possibly unique) among religious detective stories is (WARNING: IF YOU HAVEN'T READ THE BOOK AND RESENT SOLUTION GIVEAWAYS, SKIP THE REST OF THIS PARAGRAPH) the choice of murderer. Surprisingly (if not quite believably) the killer proves to be a member of the clergy—no, not a criminal disguised as a priest as in Chesterton's "The Blue Cross" but a real Roman Catholic monk. The main clue in pinning the crime on Prior Simon is Con's knowledge of his own frailty.

The strong ecumenical message makes this novel more interesting religiously than most of the others, albeit not completely successful as fiction. Among the Randollph novels, I would rank it second only to *Wages of Sin*.

Sadly, *Reverend Randollph and the Splendid Samaritan* (1986) was not quite completed when Charles Merrill Smith died in 1985. His son, Terrence Lore

Smith, who was already established as a mystery writer before his father first wrote about Randollph, completed the book and vowed to continue the Randollph series. (The younger Smith published only one solo Randollph novel, 1988's *Reverend Randollph and the Modern Miracles*, before his own untimely death in a traffic accident in the same year.)

The prologue, which occurs 25 years before the main action of the book, finds the partners in a corporation cheating the inventor of a revolutionary oil-drilling tool out of his proper share. In the present, Big Al Evans, lawyer for the partners, dies in Houston of a heart attack while being questioned (and tortured) by someone wanting to avenge the dead inventor. Evans is left with a bloody hundred-dollar bill between his hands, which have been wired together as if in prayer.

We meet Randollph reluctantly attending a prayer breakfast sponsored by the Business Executives for Christ, whose revered founder and president, Jim Trent, is the Splendid Samaritan of the title. Later Trent is murdered in the same setup as Big Al.

The sixth Randollph novel is not a particularly strong entry. One thing Smith never learned was how to reestablish his scene and cast without a lot of repetition from book to book. Again, we get a potted history of the Church of the Good Shepherd. Again, we get flashbacks to Con's first meetings with Sam and Clarence.

We also get a case of pastoral cold feet. When Randollph, who was drinking in the airport bar in his first scene in the first book, breaks with church tradition to host an open (pent)house for his parishioners, no booze is served!

In a sub-plot, Dan Gantry, the left-leaning hippyish associate pastor who appears in every book but never emerges as a truly vivid character, breaks the jaw of an attacker while participating in an antinuclear demonstration. His principal opponent on the church board is much too broad a caricature, as is often true of the antagonists in Smith's novels.

It is not specified at what point Terrence Lore Smith took over the writing. My guess would be around page 186. The style seems to change subtly, and the melodramatic gathering-of-the-suspects finale and the cutesy naming of a law firm Stout, Wodehouse, and Simenon don't sound like the elder Smith.

In summary, the Randollph books were a very likeable and enjoyable series, highlighted by the ideas and humor of the author. While the secondary characters are seldom more than cardboard, the character of the sleuth himself seems to deepen in complexity and humanity as the series goes on, and some of his regular associates at least retain their entertainment value. After the first book, Smith was weakest on puzzle and construction, a forgivable failing he has in common with several other authors of religious detective stories.

In advancing Randollph as the Protestant equivalent of Father Brown and Rabbi Small, it is important to emphasize that in the Randollph books, religion is always central to the plot and the theme. This was not generally true of earlier Protestant clergy detectives. And for all his unconventionality, vanity, and worldliness—even the spelling of his name is an affectation—Randollph emerges as a genuine clergyman. Indeed Maryell Cleary, in her essay "Contemporary Clergy Detectives" (*The Mystery Fancier*, May/June 1987), credits Smith's series with something Kemelman offers but Chesterton certainly does not: a detailed picture of the clergyperson's day-to-day duties:

> Randollph writes columns for the church newsletter, marries people, visits hospital patients, counsels those in pain, chooses hymns, decides what to preach on and writes his sermons, says the blessing at various civic events, meets with committees and the governing board, and so on, almost ad infinitum. ... Anyone considering the ministry as a career would do worse than read the Randollph books to see what it's really like—except for the murders (page 17).

Though William David Spencer, in his considerable discussion of the Randollph series, has a problem with Smith's satire, seeing a tendency to "scorch believers," he ultimately gives Smith and Randollph a favorable notice:

> Few Christian writers actively help us look above the pimps, the pushers, and the hustlers to see the pastor—a consciousness-raising that is the goal of every authentic city minister. In the virile, thoroughly attractive, and intelligent clerical hunk Randollph, Charles Merrill Smith at his best moments elevated our gaze to what God sees in everyone who serves heaven on earth—a potential champion (page 286).

Con Randollph represents the main-line Protestant churches. His theology is solid but undeniably liberal and tolerant of differences. His is the sort of church that has steadily lost membership through the 1980s, while the more conservative and fundamentalist churches have gained membership. Is it possible for a series detective to emerge from evangelical Protestantism? It is, though the character will not necessarily be a member of the clergy.

Few writers of religious detective fiction

discussed in this volume—even including writers like Chesterton, Kemelman, and Smith to whom religious ponderings were of primary interest—would claim they wrote to gain converts for their respective faiths. But in recent years, there have been examples of detective fiction, usually from Christian publishers, written from a perspective of evangelicalism and addressed either to a specifically or to a <u>potentially</u> born-again Christian readership. One recent example is John Evangelist Walsh's *The Man Who Buried Jesus* (1989), a one-of-a-kind *tour de force* which retells the story of Christ's death and burial as a detective story.

An author of more conventional mysteries is Thomas Brace Haughey, author of five novels about an evangelical equivalent of the Holmes/Watson team, Geoffrey Weston and John Taylor, the first of which, *The Case of the Invisible Thief* (1978), is discussed at some length by Ray B. Browne in "Sherlock Holmes as Christian Detective," included in his 1986 essay collection, *Heroes and Humanities: Detective Fiction and Culture*. Browne writes, "His tilt is openly four-square and born-again Christianity. His points are made in uppercase emphasis. But there is general geniality about this Holmes-Watson pair which in some ways is as pleasant as the originals.... All in all, the book is an amusing and pleasant experience" (page 132). All of Haughey's mysteries were published by a religious publisher, Bethany Fellowship. According to Allen J. Hubin's indispensable crime fiction bibliography, the most recent was *The Case of the Hijacked Moon* (1981).

Gaylord Larsen is a Christian writer who started in strictly religious markets and has to an extent bridged the gap with secular publishers. Larsen's books tend to look like spy or adventure novels, but they are more properly pure classical whodunits, often with delightfully over-elaborate and improbable puzzle edifices in the best Golden-Age tradition. He favors institutional settings (a college or university, a think tank, a movie studio) and often has some scientific interest (like DNA or plate tectonics) involved in the story. A talented writer and devious plotter, strong on prose style and characterization, Larsen could be enjoyed by a religiously indifferent audience—indeed, one of his books, *A Paramount Kill* (1988), is a strictly secular Hollywood mystery with Raymond Chandler as the main character. But in the four novels discussed below, Larsen has maintained his Christian intent while modifying his approach in interesting ways.

Larsen's first novel, *The Kilbourne Connection* (1980), was published, like all of Haughey's work, by Bethany Fellowship. The attractive front cover of the rack-sized paperback doesn't show its religious colors; the tagline under the title reads, "A former CIA investigator uncovers a heinous plot involving genetic manipulation." The back cover, though, says the book "is a vehicle not only for a heady adventure but also for a clear-cut statement of the gospel."

When former State Department employee Vern McCarthy offers 52-year-old retired CIA agent Henry Garrott a consultancy with a think tank called the Kilbourne Group, Henry initially refuses because he has become a Christian and "won't operate the way we did sometimes" (page 9). Henry's born-again experience, the result of being invited by a Congressman to a Washington, D.C. Bible study, had not immediately relieved him of all problems. He was committed to a mental institution when he started tearfully witnessing to co-workers over lunch, and not all of Henry's family shares his new-found religious enlightenment. His wife Valery remains a non-Christian (by his definition, not hers), while his college-age daughter Becky is becoming more religious as a result of her scientific studies. As the book goes on, Becky is much more given to spouting evangelical party-line clichés than her father is. Larsen clearly realizes a central character who is too lockstep pious is likely to lose the reader, especially the religiously uncommitted one.

Henry, who has an accounting background, is finally convinced to accept the assignment and journey to the think tank's headquarters in the coastal art and fishing community of Almaden, California. The Kilbourne Group's bank account is leaking funds, and they have no accountant—in an odd arrangement, the various scholars take turns keeping track of the books. Matters become more serious than theft when Dr. Robinson, one of the scholars, described by the old-fashioned term "mulatto," is murdered. The principal suspect is Professor Shoemaker, who is engaged in genetic research suggesting blacks have lower intelligence than whites, a project that poses an obvious public relations problem for the Kilbourne Center.

Writing fiction for a conservative religious publisher gives the author a different set of constraints. Larsen describes a dinner party given by McCarthy and his wife for Henry and another couple from the think tank. There are many references to the elaborate menu but no mention of pre-dinner drinks or wine with dinner, seemingly a natural part of full-scale entertaining in a secular setting. (Or even in a more liberal religious setting: there are few abstainers among the religious detectives of fiction.) I was waiting to see if Henry would forgo alcohol as a concomitant of his conversion, but he never had the chance. Did Larsen (who certainly addressed booze head-on in his secular mystery about Raymond Chandler) have to eliminate all mention of alcohol consumption to conform to the publisher's policy? The omission stands out like a sore thumb. That none of the characters uses even the mildest profanity is an easier convention to accept, especially to anyone who enjoys old movies made under the Production Code.

Larsen's first novel is readable enough but ultimately incredible. There's a touch of conspiracy/science fiction in the solution, involving DNA, genetic research, and a plot to wipe out black people all over the earth. The book ends with Henry getting a call from his old CIA chief, setting the stage for a much better second case.

Trouble Crossing the Pyrenees (1983) sees some changes. Larsen has a new publisher, Regal Books, the book division of Gospel Light Publications, and the format is now trade paperback. Henry's last name is a more conventional Garrett. Following a prologue, action begins where the previous book left off, with Henry telling wife Valery of the call from his former boss. The problem involves a team of geologists who want to hang onto a CIA monitoring device they've found a new use for. Henry wants to take the assignment because one of the geologists is a friend of his estranged son Philip. Henry's stressful relations with Valery over religious matters are emphasized more than in the first book. She sees his conversion experience as something that will eventually pass, comparable to a bad cold.

The locale is El Rio University, where Pangbourne, the chief of the geological expedition is found dead in a stock at the college renaissance fair. Arrested for the crime is Jeremy Bruce, son Philip's roommate, an exuberant "Praise the Lord"-shouting Christian and a creation scientist. Henry initially sees the whole creation/evolution controversy as beside the point, and one wonders where Larsen is going with the subject. Will Henry wind up embracing creationism? Where the novel will come down in the evolutionist/creationist debate is as suspenseful as the mystery of whodunit.

Some discussion of the solution is necessary here. (WARNING!) The crime is motivated by the desire of scientists to suppress scientific evidence supporting the creationist theory. The solution thus strikes at the very core of science-religion conflict from a fundamentalist Christian perspective.

Larsen's second novel represents an advance over his first (among other ways) in that the religious material is more fully integrated with the mystery. The plot of *The Kilbourne Connection* could easily have been used in a purely secular thriller. Not so the plot here. There are some unresolved conflicts at the end, no neat and tidy resolution. The novel is an impressive performance, whether you agree with the underlying theme (the resistance of science to challenge) or not. The novel won the Christian Fiction of the Year Award from *Cornerstone* magazine.

After *Trouble Crossing the Pyrenees* (reprinted as *An Educated Death*), Larsen changed publishers again, moving to a religiously oriented line from a mainstream publisher, Ballantine/Epiphany, and changing series characters. As *The 180-Degree Murder* (1987) opens, Trinity University psychology professor Dr. Alexander Hacchi has died an apparent suicide and President Rollins and members of the Social Science Division faculty are discussing the choice of his successor. It develops Dean Kitteridge has already invited Jason Bradley to come from Berkeley to take the job. The president, concerned with Trinity's status as a Christian institution, says, "I wonder if anything good could come out of Berkeley" (page 9)—that the statement is a biblical in-joke is immediately underlined.

From the outset, it appears someone is out to get Jason. In one of his first classes, he switches on a VCR to show a tape on psychology and finds a porno tape rolls in its place. The incident causes him to be called on the carpet by the unsympathetic president, who was suspicious of him to begin with.

Bradley is uncommitted religiously. Thus, one question is whether he will in fact be converted to Christianity, a quite different situation from presenting an already born-again sleuth as in the Henry Garrett books. Though the religious perspective remains, its expression becomes more subtle, and the secular reader is more likely to enter and receive the message.

At one point Dean Kitteridge has to inform Jason the president is asking "all new and untenured employees ... to sign a declaration of faith letter.... The letter is supposed to assure the Administration of each instructor's Christian commitment" (page 86). Kitteridge realizes Jason will be reluctant to sign a prepared letter and suggests he write a declaration of his own. Jason replies that he doubts he could come up with anything acceptable: "This whole loving and caring heavenly Father bit doesn't wash. If He's so loving and caring, why are there so many people slipping through His fingers and getting bashed on the hard pavements?" (page 90).

Near the end of the book, Jason wants to stay on at Trinity. "I'd like to be a part of a community like this," he tells Kitteridge. "I know my motivations may not be as pure and noble as yours or others who are dedicated Christians. But I'd like to live my life as though it were true. Does that sound artificial? Maybe so, but it's the best I can offer right now" (page 249).

The Dean keeps plugging away, comparing Jason's favorite sport of hang-gliding with Christianity: "A person who has never done it might even say it could be disastrous to jump off such a high cliff into nothing. But the experienced flyer has faith. He's been there before, and he knows he can trust himself to the wind, even though he can't see it" (page 250).

As a detective novel, *The 180-Degree Murder* gives full value in complex plot and action. But, as with the books about Henry Garrett, the second is a considerable advance over the first.

Atascadero Island (1989), another classical detective story with an adventure-story title, begins with a dying message designed to get readers running to their Bibles: an elderly archaeologist, stabbed to death, writes in blood "Rom. 15:24," then puts a line through it with his fingernail. Jason Bradley, in Switzerland on a bicycling tour, is invited to the Balaeric Islands off the coast of Spain by a representative of televangelist Reverend Bobby Carmichael, star of the glitzy "Time of Praise" program, who wants his services as a forensic psychologist. Larsen's description of one of the "Time of Praise" broadcasts is a wickedly accurate depiction (without much satirical exaggeration necessary) of evangelical showbiz. Still, Carmichael is one of the most interesting of the many televangelists in recent mystery fiction: though certainly not an admirable or attractive character, he is not a pure charlatan either. His faith and belief seem to be real despite his skewed priorities and his longing to be a "religious superstar" like the Pope or Billy Graham.

The novel's McGuffin is a typical one in religious and literary detective stories: the lost manuscript, in this case a new Pauline letter, which (shockingly) seems to portray Paul as succumbing to his doubts.

Atascadero Island is Larsen's best book to date. It has a fine puzzle, highlighted by a masterfully fair central clue and a good piece of mystery misdirection, pointing to one innocent suspect with two standard detective novel indicators. Avoiding pat theological answers, the story effectively drives home the theme that Jason Bradley spells out: that Christianity "has to stand in the spotlight of examination and testing just like everything else in man's experience ... If God is really there and Jesus is who he says he is, then the truth will come out, despite the obstacles" (page 119).

A second secular Larsen novel, forthcoming as this is written, has what the author calls "a certain cross-over with the religious market." *Dorothy and Agatha* (1990) involves Sayers and Christie in a joint detecting role. Sayers, of course, left the mystery field in part to serve as a popular Christian playwright and apologist.

What is the future of the Protestant religious detective story as we enter the 1990s? With religious settings and situations figuring more and more prominently in detective fiction generally, it seems likely another clergy detective will emerge to fill the gap left by the end of the Reverend Randollph series. Possibly Isabelle Holland's Claire Aldington, now the most prominent Protestant clergyperson sleuth, will achieve new popularity. Whether the specifically evangelical detective story is sufficiently commercially viable to proliferate remains to be seen—Christian book dealers have generally found fiction a far harder sell than non-fiction—but whether in a religious or a secular arena, writers like Gaylord Larsen can be expected to continue to deliver their message of faith.

RELIGIOUS CULTS AND THE MYSTERY

by Marvin Lachman

Religious detectives who are priests, rabbis, nuns, and ministers have long been mainstays of the mystery genre. Father Brown, Rabbi Small, Sister Ursula, the Reverend Randollph, and many others are not only equipped to deal with spiritual needs, but they also have the insight and intelligence to solve crimes. However, there is a reverse side to religion in the mystery, and a surprisingly large number of books and stories depend on cults which are by their nature *irreligious*, with leaders who prey upon their flocks for power and/or financial gain.

The popularity of the religious cult as a mystery plot device is an outgrowth of the rise of cults, especially in England and California, between the World Wars. In 1928, A.E.W. Mason, one of the most successful novelists of the detective story's "Golden Age," gave his series characters, Hanaud and Ricardo, in *The Prisoner in the Opal*, a case involving murder and the Black Mass in the South of France. Mason has Hanaud, with sympathy and humor, trace the origins of these ceremonies:

> 'The old Sabbaths—one can understand them better. Poor serfs, hungry, without pleasures, in revolt against the great injustice which gave all the colour of the world to a handful of nobles and all the misery of the world to the rest.... No wonder they danced furiously, those poor people in their forest glades. No wonder the first in favour was the one who danced

faster than the others. They had to keep warm.'

But Hanaud has no sympathy for rituals as practiced in the twentieth century. "That's sheer decadence. The people of disappointed ambitions, those who have exhausted the normal joys and crave the forbidden ones, those who would sell their immortal souls for a new thrill, those who look to Satan for the gifts which Christ refuses." Mason uses surprisingly erotic language for his times as he puts sexuality at the core of these rites:

> ... the orgy. ... the frenzy of the adoration of Satan which in half an hour would make of that room a stew, a sty of animals met in a battle of lust ... As the sacred climax approached, a great trembling took her body and limbs, her eyes opened and fixed themselves on the Adonis, cries uttered low, like the whimperings of an animal, broke continually from her lips.

Ngaio Marsh's cult in *Death in Ecstasy* (1936) is tame compared to Mason's. She even provides a disclaimer, saying,

> In case the House of the Sacred Flame might be thought to bear a superficial resemblance to any existing church or institution, I hasten to say that if any similarity exists, it is purely fortuitous. The House of the Sacred Flame, its officials, and its congregation are all imaginative and exist only in Knocklatchers Row.

Roderick Alleyn's reporter friend Nigel Bathgate attends one of their services, noting the use of zodiac signs, priestly robes of a Druidical cut, and the hypnotizing speech of the leader, the Reverend Jasper

Religious Cults and the Mystery

Garnette, who relies on staging with candlelight to dramatize his appearance. Nothing too exotic happens during the service until, when the sacred wine cup is passed to a wealthy initiate, she falls unconscious. Garnette claims she is in spiritual ecstasy, but she actually has been fatally poisoned, and Alleyn is called. Garnette says, "Our ceremony of the Cup, though it embraces the virtues of various communions in Christian churches, is actually entirely different in essentials and in intention." Alleyn, though not a believer in organized religion, replies coldly, "I was not so mistaken as to suspect any affinity."

Spinsters in Jeopardy (1953), atypical Marsh because it is a thriller, involves "strange hybrid cults made up from shreds of genuine religions ... supported and maintained by the use of drugs." In disguise, Alleyn attends one of their ceremonies, sneaking in his own tobacco cigarettes so he will not have to partake of the "reefers" they are passing around. He observes an Egyptian-type ceremony of "unbridled phallicism" in which the word "Ra" is repeated over and over by the initiates, "who began to bark it out with an enthusiasm, Alleyn thought, only to be equalled by the organized cheers of an American ball game."

Another British detective story writer became so identified with the occult in the mystery that a series of reprints called "The Dennis Wheatley Library of the Occult" was published. Wheatley created Neils Orsen, a Swede, who is billed as "the world's greatest psychic investigator" though the solutions in his "Ghost Hunter" stories never involve truly rational explanations. An early Wheatley novel, *The Devil Rides Out* (1935), can be read as a warning against dabbling in the occult, but such was the climate of opinion in England at the time that, instead, it evoked letters from readers who were quick to claim various psychic experiences. Wheatley's anthology, *Gunmen, Gallants, and Ghosts* (1943), contains many short stories and articles which deal with the occult and his researches into it. He found Satanism practiced through the world with "women giving themselves up to hideous eroticism with a great carved ebony figurine during Satanic orgies held in a secret temple in London's Bayswater district." Calling the Black Mass "a perversion of Christianity ... a complete travesty of the Christian ritual and the supreme act in the worship of the Devil," Wheatley advises readers who have been touched by these rituals, "Should you ever have reason to believe that you or yours have come into the orbit of malignant occult forces, do not hesitate to consult your parson or priest. They will not laugh. And should you ever be confronted with an evil manifestation, have no fear. Pray for help."

Colonel Verney, a Wheatley series character employed by British Intelligence, gets involved in cases in which the occult, as well as espionage, are important, e.g., *To the Devil a Daughter* (1953) and *The Satanist* (1960), a book worth considering because it is one of a small sub-genre which links Russian communism and cults. It also achieves the status of what Bill Pronzini would call "an alternate classic."

Verney is convinced that Russia is attempting to infiltrate the British Labour Party and that one of his own operatives, Teddy Morden, was the victim of a ritual murder while investigating this. Morden's widow volunteers to help investigate the Brotherhood of Ram, a theosophist group which Verney is sure is a communist front. Sex ("unbridled lust, perversion and obscenity") is a major part of the ritual of the group and Mary Morden is made to participate in orgies. The group's leader (The Great Ram) is really Otto Khune, a German atomic scientist. Other leaders include both Asian and American Indians, giving Wheatley the opportunity to have his characters display some of the racist attitudes shown by the creations of H.C. McNeile and Sydney Horler more than twenty years before. The Great Ram has an atom bomb at his disposal and is willing to risk World War III to achieve his ends, telling Mary, "Since you have shown yourself to be one of those who follow the pathetic slave religion started by the imposter Christ, it pleases me that you should hear me announce the death knell of Christianity." Those words signal one of the wildest climaxes in the history of mystery fiction.

Colin Watson's *Kissing Covens* (1972) is as much satire as detective story, beginning with a hilarious description of a group of middle-aged residents of Flaxborough conducting their midnight St. Walpurga Eve ceremony. The evening chill, plus vestiges of modesty, causes most of the group to eschew nudity in favor of such variegated garments as bathing suits, khaki shorts, woolen drawers, brassieres, and even a fur coat. Most of the group gets drunk on cheap wine and "do their own thing. It was clear that the ceremony, although not yet at an end, had entered the phase of independent interpretation." One member, Mrs. Pentatuke, does finally dance nude. The group, called the Sabbath Day Conservation Society, is really rather conservative during daylight hours, even using Robert's Rules for their meetings. The president of the society is shocked by Mrs. Pentatuke's actions which she describes as "terribly carnal. I think she must have something wrong with her glands."

At first Inspector Purbright has a tendency to ignore the group. Later, he sounds like Noel Coward as he responds to newspaper questions as to whether the police are concerned about black magic in the community, saying, "I would prefer to be allowed the middle course of benevolent agnosticism; tell me where a black mass is going on and I'll see if there's anything we can or ought to do about it." However, murder and the desecration of a local church force Purbright to take things more seriously. Watson paints his "amateur satanists" with a jaundiced eye and seems to parody Wheatley when he has one character declare that the Russians organized the establishment of witch covens in England and America as a part of an onslaught on the Christian world.

By the 1980s cults in the mystery had taken on a regrettable blandness. Witness John Greenwood's *Mists Over Mosley* (1986), an otherwise delightful British country mystery, in which an under-sized coven of only three women contrives what appears to be witchcraft in order to combat local political corruption. As an example of just how domesticized religious cults had become, we have one of the women saying jokingly, "Cauldrons are out. We do our newts' eyes in a micro-wave oven nowadays."

In the United States religious cults figured so strongly in the pulp magazines of the 1920s and 1930s that one critic suggested, only partly in jest, a pulp called *Black Mass*. Beginning in 1925 Seabury Quinn wrote 93 short stories about Jules de Grandin, formerly of Lê Sureté. Fifty years later, when Popular Library reprinted several collections of these, they advertised de Grandin as "The Occult Hercule Poirot and A Sherlock of the Supernatural." Functioning out of the prosaic fictional town of Harrisonville, New Jersey, with the help of the Watson-like Dr. Trowbridge, de Grandin solves many weird mysteries, occasionally using legitimate detection as he takes on vampires, werewolves, and diabolism.

The most memorable Quinn is the novel *The Devil's Bride*, originally serialized in 1932 in five issues of *Weird Tales*. De Grandin is called in because "spreading like a soul-destroying cancer over all the earth were cells of the Devil-worshipping organization that hungered for supreme power over humans - and used both the dark forces of the spirit and the most seductive female flesh to gain its diabolical ends." Quinn was probably the first writer to link religious cults to Russia, having them supply money to a Satan-worshipping sect he calls "this league of Godlessness which is a poisonous fungus spreading throughout the world from that cellar of unclean abominations we call Russia."

In disguise, de Grandin and Trowbridge enter the cult chapel and view a ceremony (amid the smell of cannabis) at which priests say, "Do what thou will; this shall be the whole of the law." The congregation intones, "Love is the law; love free and unbound." A convert, "stripped of her enshrouding veils, clad only in her own white beauty" is branded with a red hot iron. A temporarily stunned de Grandin whispers, "Morbleu ... Can such things be?" before taking his customary decisive action.

While Quinn was achieving popularity, A. Merritt achieved even greater success with *Seven Footprints to Satan*, a five-part mystery in the July 2nd through August 1st 1927 issue of *Argosy All-Story Magazine.* The following year it was republished in book form and has seldom been out of print since. Explorer James Kirkham is kidnapped on a New York subway and taken to the headquarters of a man who calls himself "Satan" and plays "chess" with real people. He forces Kirkham to play a deadly game involving seven steps, a parody on organized religion, leading to "Satan's throne." The price of defeat: Kirkham's life and liberty. "Satan" is surrounded by fabulous wealth and many slaves. He also has other victims imprisoned, including Eve Demerest, a lovely woman with whom Kirkham falls in love.

Some have said that in his first novel, *Red Harvest*, Dashiell Hammett intended to show capitalism run wild. A similar hypothesis is that his second, *The Dain Curse* (first published in the Nov. 1928-Feb. 1929 issues of *Black Mask*), is the author's indictment of religion. The Continental Op, hired to find diamonds stolen from wealthy inventor Edgar Leggett, is quickly diverted to searching for Leggett's young daughter, Gabrielle, who has disappeared. He rescues her from the Temple of the Holy Grail, a well-financed religious cult which occupies a six-story building in "a good San Francisco residential neighborhood." The temple, founded by a former actor, Joseph Haldorn, has a large following among the city's elite.

Gabrielle, with her doctor's consent, returns to the Temple for "rest and psychic recovery," though the Op accompanies her. Soon she is found with a bloody dagger, standing over the corpse of the doctor. Later, Haldorn, in love with Gabrielle, attempts to murder his wife on the altar of the temple, "believing himself a stern unyielding god endowed with the power to take away life." So possessed is he that it takes the Op seven bullets and, finally, a knife to stop him! With the temple behind her, Gabrielle marries and moves to the shore, but the Op is called back when her young husband is drowned, and finally he solves the Dain curse.

Lesser known writers than Hammett filled the pages of what seemed an almost endless number of pulps, and a significant percentage of their words involved religious cults. According to the title page blurbs the first issue of *Thrilling Mystery* included stories which told how: 1. "A Satanic Spirit Spreads Havoc in an Unholy Campaign of Destruction." 2. "Madness Rules a Crypt of Corruption Where Dead Mouths Are Sated with Dripping Flesh." 3. "A Greed-Crazed Maniac Sets the Stage for a Horrifying Orgy of Human Sacrifice."

Certain themes seemed to appeal to readers of cult stories, and these were repeated many times, with minor variation. A favorite was the attractive young couple, often on their honeymoon, beset by apparently unexplainable horror, though usually greed or insane jealousy, rather than anything supernatural, is responsible. Paul Ernst was one of the best at using this device. In his "The Thing Behind the Iron Door" (*Horror Stories*, Oct.-Nov. 1937) a young couple rents a house and is terrorized by the reincarnation of Indra, the Mayan rain god, who turns out to be their real estate agent coveting the young wife. Ernst's "Man into Monster" (*Terror Tales* Aug. 1935) confronts the hero with a situation in which his sweetheart's father, a professor of Egyptology, is suffering from a mysterious malady which is transforming him, in some reverse Darwinian process, into an ape. He investigates and finds that the professor's assistant, obsessed with the professor's daughter, has caused the ailment through an ancient ritual. In "The Devil at the Wheel" (*Thrilling Mystery* Jan. 1936) a busload of people is kidnapped and driven to what appears to be the River Styx, complete with Satan and his imps cavorting. The villain has staged this whole event to create an atmosphere which will frighten people away so that he can obtain rights to land rich in natural gas and oil. Ernst even had a series character, Dr. Satan, who appeared regularly in *Weird Tales* and was billed as "the world's weirdest criminal."

When members of a family die off in H.M. Appel's "Blood Feast" (*Dime Mystery* Mar. 1935), the curse of a storm god is blamed, but it is really the insanely jealous architect who built their mansion and creeps through its secret passageways. The mysterious illness suffered by a young teacher in Hugh B. Cave's "School Mistress for the Mad" (*Sinister Stories* Apr. 1940) is caused by the ritualistic experiments of a local doctor.

Though suspense and the "everyday going wrong" was the hallmark of Cornell Woolrich's work, he occasionally delved into the more exotic, using religious cults. "Baal's Daughter" (*Thrilling Mystery* Jan. 1936) has Bob Collins and his fiancée, Gloria, as prisoners of Dr. Dessaw, a psychiatrist who is really the leader of the cult of Ishtar. (Dessaw's assistant walks around with a panther to which she feeds human meat.) Bob is chained to the wall and forced to watch a ceremony in which Gloria will become the sacrifice of Baal and then fed to the panther. It's a perfect opportunity for some of the Woolrichian prose that has made generations of readers either love or hate his work: "The cords of my neck swelled with pressure of raging blood. My pulses beat like tom-toms at my temples, in my eyes, hammered behind my ears. Every muscle in my body seemed to crack with tension as I strained against the wall."

Bud Ingram in Woolrich's "Graves for the Living" (*Dime Mystery* June 1937) has developed a phobia about people being buried alive. When he was young, his father had been buried alive due to negligence on the part of the medical examiner and the mortician. Bud even goes to cemeteries and warns people at services, "Make sure he's dead!" Despite this behavior, Joan Blaine, whom he meets at one of these funerals, falls in love with him. She tries to make him less morbid, but he continues to visit graveyards and discovers a group called "The Friends of Death" which bilks wealthy, ill people by promising to keep them alive after burial. Bud and Joan are captured by the group, and she *is* buried alive. Bud escapes and goes to the police for help but finds those in charge may be members of the Friends. (The story, told in flashback, opens with Bud walking into the police station saying he is looking for his fiancée's grave. Asked when she died, he replies, "She didn't die.")

There is another doctor involved in weird events in the small town of Milo in "Plague of the Black Passion" which Bruno Fischer wrote under his Russell Gray pseudonym for *Horror Stories* Aug.-Sept. 1939. Gregory Flood visits his fiancée and finds that most of the women in town are suffering from the unlikely combination of black plague and insatiable lust. In another marvelously "grabbing" opening, Flood finds himself blamed by the men for what has occurred: "They were waiting for me at the station, those grim-faced men with the look of fear and murder in their eyes.... We want you, Gregory Flood. We're going to string you up.... The devil has possessed the womenfolk of Milo, and you opened the gate to let him in." Flood must save himself and also find the medical reasons for the sickness which has overtaken the women.

Often in cult stories the elderly are portrayed as evil, preying upon the young. In another Fischer-Gray story, "Burn-Lovely Lady" (*Dime Mystery* June 1938), a young bride is captured and tortured by "cackling, obscene-minded old men and women." In Nat Schachner's "Monsters of the Pit" (*Terror Tales* Nov. 1934), a honeymoon couple in the Canadian north is kidnapped and dragged to an underground lair where a false priest prepares to torture the bride, tearing off her clothes while his Neanderthal-type helpers dance around in glee. Shortly after the couple in Arthur J. Burks' "Devils in the Dust" (*Thrilling Mystery* Dec. 1935) are married, they find that the preacher who married them is a madman, leader of a cult group which had delved into old, forbidden religions "until sadism and brutality became their fundamentals of faith." The groom's priority is preventing the preacher from attacking his bride.

Egyptology in the pulps was often synonymous with evil. In Wayne Rogers' "Tomorrow They Die" (*Mystery Adventures* Mar. 1935), the villain lures young women to a private lodge where senile, tubercular men live under his charge. Knowing they are near death, they willingly pay large sums of money for the women. After ceremonies involving flogging and a Black Mass, they die off after arranging that their young "brides" are buried alive in their coffins, as they believe was the Egyptian custom. Richard B. Sale, a prolific and usually intelligent pulp writer, used Egyptology to explain the actions of his beautiful villainess in "Rescued by Satan" (*Mystery Adventures* May 1936). She is fulfilling an old superstition which permits her to be normal eleven months of the year but during the twelfth turns her into a human tiger, with a fierce urge to kill.

The two "V's," vampirism and voodooism, were frequently used in the pulps, with Cornell Woolrich probably writing the best stories on each theme. "Vampire's Honeymoon" (*Horror Stories* Aug.-Sept. 1939) creates so believable a world that one almost believes there *are* vampires. Dick Manning, a wealthy young man, is happily engaged until at his engagement party he is kissed by a vampire named Faustine. The story telling encourages suspension of disbelief as it tells of Dick's fight against becoming a vampire, himself: "Night and mystery seemed to be calling to me ... as though some occult power were pulling at me, guiding my footsteps toward it ..."

Woolrich's "Holocaust" (*Argosy* Dec. 12, 1936) is set in Haiti and makes use of native belief in zombies while he tells of a 19th century slave revolt. His voodoo classic, however, is "Dark Melody of Death" (*Dime Mystery* July 1935) about Eddie Bloch, a white orchestra leader, who hears a voodoo chant and partakes in an initiation ceremony so he can write down the music. His rendition of the chant becomes a tremendous hit, making him the most popular band leader in New Orleans. Bloch, losing weight and becoming weak for no apparent reason, is convinced that the cult he joined has placed a curse on him. With the help of a Cajun detective, Jacques Desjardin, he breaks up the group and its leader, Papa Benjamin, but now Bloch is faced with the life-or-death choice of whether he dares have his band play the chant which made them successful.

Frank Kane, a mystery novelist who started writing for the pulps, wrote *Poisons Unknown* (1952), one of the few mystery novels on the subject of voodooism. Kane's private eye, Johnny Liddell, is in New Orleans to investigate a cult, "The Eye Almighty," which has gotten prominent people to participate in their rituals and then blackmailed them. The group is run by Brother Alfred, but its real attraction is the high priestess, Wanda, and she is "performing" the evening Liddell visits their tabernacle. Wanda begins singing and then falls under a spell.

> Wildly, she tore at her clothes, ripped them from her body. She danced wildly, her hair flying, her body undulating and throbbing in time with the music. Her motions became more and more frantic until suddenly, with a wild scream, she collapsed in a heap on the floor and lay there. That was a signal for the whole line of marchers to take up her dance. The drumbeat speeded up in intensity; the motions of the dancers kept time. The women tore at their clothes, and entirely nude, went on dancing.

(They all had been drinking a wine spiked with hashish.) Afterward, when he is asked for his impression of the ceremony, Liddell replies, in a masterpiece of understatement, "It's not exactly a way to grow old gracefully, is it?"

With his narrative abilities and sense of humor, Richard S. Prather would have been the ideal pulp writer, but he began his career just when those magazines were dying off. His *Dead Man's Walk* (1965) is one of the most enjoyable mysteries dealing with voodooism, and Prather even lets his hero Shell Scott display some of his creator's research on the subject.

> In reading of Verde I'd come across

much about the basic religion of the island, *voudon* or voodooism - much like the Haitian variety, but with indigenous corruption and invention. Plus a liberal addition of sorcery, black magic and such. As to why the natives are afraid of voodoo and, especially *zombies* (the living dead), it's a fear with its roots stretching back centuries, back into old Africa - that's where voodoo was born.

Scott is on the fictional Caribbean island of Verde because of murder at a new luxury hotel. A corrupt voodoo priest named Count Mordieux is threatening to have all the workers quit their jobs. Scott, believing the murder and labor unrest are related, attends various voodoo rites. He also attends a sexy show at a local night club which ends with the obligatory nude scene, but he is prevented from fully enjoying it when he is taken ill after a pin is stuck into a voodoo doll created in his image. A native girl gives him a local preparation which cures him, and he resolves the case after attending, in disguise, the ceremony in The Valley of the Dead. He leaves for his home in Los Angeles, feeling he has fully earned the sobriquet "Shell Scott, white witch doctor."

While the pulps were filling page after page with stories about cults, a few Eastern mystery writers inserted them into novels. Though writers like Ellery Queen and Clayton Rawson wrote some of the most bizarre detective stories published, they were never as successful at integrating religious cults, even into their best books. Queen's *The Egyptian Cross Mystery* (1932) begins impressively with a crucifixion in rural West Virginia, and its combination of exotic mystery and fair play detection made it the choice of some critics as the best of Queen's early novels. The book's weakest portion involves a man who calls himself "Harakht, the Sun God" and operates a nudist colony

Religious Cults and the Mystery

on Oyster Island in Long Island Sound. He even speaks ancient Egyptian; he was Stryker, one of the world's greatest Egyptologists before he apparently went insane. Queen describes Harakht as "a little old man unkempt and brown-bearded, with fanatical eyes. He was swathed in a pure white robe. He wore curious sandals." The description seems surprisingly cliched because many cult leaders have been so depicted, but Queen's word picture predated most of them.

Clayton Rawson, himself a magician, has his series detective, The Great Merlini, investigate deaths that appear to be the result of witchcraft in *Death from a Top Hat* (1938). The first victim is Dr. Sabbat, a student of demonology and the occult. He is found

> on his back, symmetrically spread-eagled in the exact center of a large star shape that had been drawn on the floor with chalk, his head, arms, and legs extending out into the points. At the tip of each point stood one of the candles and around this whole fantastic tableau ran a scribbled border of strange words like *Tetragrammaton.*

Sabbat had claimed to have supernatural powers and had written of such cultish subjects as vampirism and lycanthropy. The second victim, Eugene Tarot, was known as "the king of cards." Both men are found in locked rooms. Rawson includes a great deal of scholarship, both real and mock, about the occult, but somehow these elements are overshadowed by his deftly placed clues, Times Square atmosphere, and humorous touches.

George Harmon Coxe was never known for writing exotic mysteries, and his religious cult in *The Groom Lay Dead* (1944) is decidedly humdrum. Only the setting is unusual for a religious cult, New York's

Finger Lakes region. A petty blackmailer, "Dr." Samson Penzance, runs a cult called the "Brotherhood of Horus," based on the Sun God of Upper Egypt. Although the group is supposed to be one of sun worshippers, they go around modestly dressed, all wearing shorts, with the women wearing halters or handkerchiefs above the waist. Penzance's philosophy includes clichés like, "many of the mysteries of life can be understood through the proper exploration of one's nature, by one's self. My purpose is to help the honest, courageous lovers of truth to achieve a greater understanding, to help them find the power of useful knowledge that has been passed down through the ages." Fortunately, Coxe is good enough at telling a story to overcome his own misguided attempt to add spice.

There must be something about the intellectual and/or physical climate of the Northeast which is inimical to religious cults, because even a book like Richard Forrest's *Lark* (1986), written during a more liberated time, fails to capture the reader's interest. Perhaps it is because Forrest's Connecticut group seems dated, as if he should have written about it in 1970 or not at all. Investigating the murder of a young woman, Tommy Lark, a tough cop, interviews the leader (Magus) of a group which has taken a house in a rundown area. The Magus (real name Winthrop) admits they hold services in the nude because "the removal of all garments means that we are all equal and free to receive the faintest of spiritual traces." Though Winthrop claims to have a coven, someone points out that he only had four members and thirteen are required. Winthrop, in embarrassment, replies, "We're working on it." As if aware that this meager cult will not sustain a novel, Forrest shifts to more trendy topics like pornography and serial killing.

Possibly the liveliest Eastern book on cults is Chester Himes' *Blind Man with a Pistol* (1969), set in

New York's Harlem. While a Grave Digger Jones-Coffin Ed Johnson detective story, it is basically about Black Power and would not qualify for an article on cults, were it not for a very amusing reference early in the book to an old man calling himself the "Reverend Sam," who lives in a decrepit building on 119th St. with twelve women and the more than fifty children he has fathered. The police are attracted when they see his sign advertising for "fertile womens" (sic). Reverend Sam dresses his women as nuns and sends them out on the streets, explaining, "there were white nuns and black nuns.... The Church provided shelter and food for the white nuns; his black nuns had to hustle for themselves...."

If the East was not a fertile breeding ground for cults, Southern California proved to be, and few mystery authors writing about the area could resist the inclusion of at least one cult. Religious cults in Southern California were often satirized in a devastating manner. Ngaio Marsh had been almost apologetic in her disclaimer compared to the disavowal of Anthony Boucher (writing as H.H. Holmes) in *Nine Times Nine* (1940): "The characters in this book are completely fictitious.... There is, at the time of writing, no cult in Los Angeles called the Temple of Light, though Lord knows that there may be before publication date." In it R. Wolf Harrigan, author of *Fleece My Sheep*, said to be the standard work on phony religious rackets, is researching a pair of cult leaders Swami Mahopadhyaya Virasenanda (born Herman Sussmaul) and Ahsaver, leader of the Temple of Light. Harrigan is impressed by the sheer theatricality of Ahsaver's church (the neon sigh proclaiming **LIGHT** can be seen ten blocks away) and his performance: "He dominated the stage and the entire auditorium ... it was even hard to guess what he actually looked like ... his face was obscured by a black, spade-shaped beard, along the Assyrian style. And his body was completely enveloped by the famous Yellow Robe."

Following the collection, Ahsaver places the titular curse, for his mockery, upon Harrigan, who is soon found murdered in a locked room. Ahsaver claims responsibility, though he has an unbreakable alibi and dares Lt. Terrence Marshall of the LAPD to arrest him. Marshall declines but then, with the aid of a series detective with real credentials in religion, Sister Ursula of the Sisters of Martha of Bethany, he discovers the murderer.

While the early pulps emphasized the weirder aspects of cults, especially heroines in danger, later stories like John K. Butler's excellent "The Saint in Silver" (*Dime Detective* Jan. 1941), used phony religion, as did Boucher, for a detective story plot device. L.A. cab driver Steve Middletown Knight ("Steve Midnight") is following the people who knocked him out and stole his evening fares. The trail leads to murder and then a fabulous mansion in Beverly Hills, the home of Saint Rufus of the Thou Shalt Society. He also visits their temple, which is even more impressive than the one Boucher imagined. It "might have been designed by a movie studio.... On the tremendous rounded dome was a colossal neon sign you could see across the roof-tops for miles two words of brooding threat - THOU SHALT."

Reflecting on the many rackets in Los Angeles, Midnight says,

> The Thou Shalt Society was one of the newer innovations. Not entirely new, of course, since for hundreds of years shady swindlers have hidden behind a mask of religion in order to ply their graft. Hallelujah, praise the Lord! Put fifty cents in the collection basket and save the immortal soul! Dig down brethren! The Thou Shalt Society was one of those. A racket plied against lonely people, against

the sick, against the worried, against the aged. The lousiest racket in the world, hiding behind a cloak of spiritual religion and defying you to prove it's just a cloak. The Thou Shalt Society preached a doctrine 'thou shalt soon die. Therefore, thou hast no need for thy earthly wealth.' Dig down, brethren.

Kenneth Millar, writing as Ross Macdonald in his first Lew Archer novel, *The Moving Target* (1949), showed himself to be a superb observer of the Southern California scene. Archer has been hired by Elaine Sampson to find her missing millionaire husband. He had given property, including a mountain and a house, to a cult called "The Temple in the Clouds." The Temple "hidden from everyone but hawks and airmen" is presided over by Claude who "wears his hair long and never cuts his beard and talks like a bad imitation of Walt Whitman." Claude, still another sun-worshipper, threatens the "Wrath of Mithras" on Archer if he tries to enter the temple since he has not been "purified." Later, when Claude is in trouble and must flee, he asks Archer what he should do and is told to "open another store-front religion." The religious charlatan is only one of many interesting characters in what was the start of one of the longest and best private eye series ever.

The approaches of Boucher and Macdonald were relatively serious compared to Prather, who wrote two devastatingly funny Shell Scott mysteries about Southern California cults, displaying his own cynicism regarding all religion. In *Always Leave 'em Dying* (1954), Scott takes a case involving a missing sixteen-year-old. He is concerned because the girl's mother forced her to join the Trammelites, which Scott considers a crackpot cult but "the biggest, best known, and most profitable" one, so successful that he believes it "might eventually succeed in disorganizing as many minds as organized religion." (Though they were at opposite ends of the political spectrum, Prather and Hammett had similar opinions about religion.) Scott describes Arthur Trammel, whose followers refer to him as "The Master" and "The All-High," as "dressed always in black, he looked like an undertaker who had embalmed himself by mistake." When Scott criticizes Trammel as a hypocrite whose appeal comes from deliberately titillating his followers by reading extensively from Henry Miller as an example of the sin he *claims* he wants to eradicate, he is attacked by a left-wing newspaper with the headline "Private Detective Runs Amuck!"

Attempting to find the girl leads Scott to a phony psychiatric hospital where he is knocked out, put in a straight jacket, and then given "an intra-vena (sic) injection." He escapes in time for a major outdoor event at which Trammel, who has been murdered (with Scott a primary suspect), is to be reborn. Scott shows up, disguised as a cult leader, "The Master of the Moon People," in a black robe and long black beard. More than fifty thousand people gather at what Scott calls "a panorama of paranoia ... many faiths were here - and thus the lack of many faiths." Present are leaders of 300 cults, and Scott finds that he has something in common with them: opposition to the Trammelites, whose success has been taking away their followers. The climax is a wild one, Prather at his best.

In *Dead-Bang* (1971) there are similarities to his earlier cult mystery, but Prather takes advantage of the sexual revolution of the 1960s. This time his target is Festus Lemming and his "Church of the Second Coming," a group Scott describes as "a collection of ecclesiastical fruitcakes that had to be described as *the* major religious success story of the twentieth century." Lemming makes use of the latest innovations, including music played with deafening acoustical amplification: "that sound, that noise, that astonishing assault on the senses, could not have been more perfectly designed to disorient the brain ... It wasn't exactly rock and roll.... It was more like rack and ruin." Lemming also uses gigantic neon signs to advertise his church, which is near one of the exit ramps on the Santa Ana Freeway. He makes extensive use of show business techniques, wearing "a simple business suit made of hammered gold with ruby crosses for buttons. Lights from spots focused upon him ... as the sun might have glinted from the chain mail of a Crusader setting forth to chop up infidels for God."

Prather has much fun with the group, inventing hymns and cheers for them, calling the followers, not surprisingly, "Lemmings" and referring to the whole enterprise as "Funland at Disneychurch." The plot (to the extent there is one) involves the kidnapping of Lemming's sworn enemy, Emmanuel Bruno, whose daughter hired Scott. Lemming claims to hate Bruno because the latter has invented Erovite, a patent medicine which seems to have aphrodisiac qualities. Of course, Lemming, though an avowed enemy of sex and sin, retains his audience by using his own erotic examples during his sermons: "the hairy thighs of lust...."

Prather, obviously having a great time, also invents bluenose groups to whom he gives acronyms such as MOMS (Mothers Opposed to Man and Sex) and NONOO (Nuns in Opposition to Nudity and Other Obscenities). He takes shots at organized religion, especially St. Paul and his preachings: "Paul had no use for the opposite sex....This was the man who offered all other men a counterfeit ticket to Heaven and asked in payment only that they surrender their manhood ... his words became sacred Scripture, with the result that for nearly two thousand years all good Christians have been robbing Peter to pay Paul." We end up with a hilarious scene in which hundreds of Lemmings chase

Scott who, unsuccessfully, wields an 80 pound cross to drive them back. He finally escapes, in a riotously funny scene, crowded into his Cadillac with ten beautiful girls who removed all their clothing as a protest against the Lemmings.

Unfortunately, all mysteries about Southern California religious cults were not as much fun. An example of one quite pedestrian is Dell Shannon's *Extra Kill* (1962), in which Luis Mendoza visits The Temple of Mystic Truth on Wilshire Boulevard while investigating blackmail. The ceremony, as described, is far from exotic, and perhaps that is why Shannon says very little money was given during the collection.

The very best writers have not only *used* cults, they have *created* entire societies within the pages of their books. A prime example is one which eschews the opportunity to make fun of its subject, Margaret Millar's *How Like an Angel* (1962). In the foreword to a 1987 reprint, Millar described how a friend suggested a book about California cults, and she had replied, "I know very little about such cults." His response was, "So, start your own," and she did within the pages of her book. Her protagonist is Joe Quinn, a compulsive gambler and sometimes private eye, who is stranded near the Tower of Heaven. Given lodging, he meets the members who carry such names as Sister Blessing of the Salvation; Brother Crown of Thorns; Brother Tongue of Prophets; and Sister Contrition. There is also The Master whom the cynical Quinn regards as "a schizo and a fear peddler. His racket's as old as the hills. It doesn't take the curse off because he believes in himself, it only makes it doubly dangerous."

Quinn accepts money from Sister Blessing (who has hidden small gifts from her son) to investigate a murder which occurred in a nearby town five years before. The past murder (and a bank robbery) turn out to be connected with murder in the Tower, and Quinn does a great deal of soul searching, as well as detective work, eventually finding that while he has affected the lives of the cult members, they have done the same for him.

If Ellery Queen did not create a very convincing cult in *The Egyptian Cross Mystery*, he did just the opposite when he wrote of Southern California in his most controversial novel, *And on the Eighth Day* (1964), set during World War II. Ellery, after writing scripts for Army training films in Hollywood, is driving across the desert and loses his way, coming upon a religious-socialist-utopian community. Queen invests an entire society with a complex set of beliefs and varied characters called The Teacher (their leader), The Slave, The Storesman, The Chronicler, The Weaver, and The Successor. They live in the valley of Quenan and when the Teacher hears Ellery's name, he believes that the visitor foretold in their sacred book has come as prophesied. The community has been living in isolation for over fifty years without any violence or knowledge of the outside world. Such are the conventions of the mystery that now one of the members is murdered, and Ellery is called upon to investigate. Here is a mystery that can be read as novel of religious metaphor (the events take place during Easter week) or as a very good, fair-play detective story.

No one can accuse that sub-genre, the religious cult mystery (especially its Southern California variety) of not having kept up with the times. It has consistently mirrored trends in society and even been prophetic. In 1955, Edward D. Hoch began his long series of stories about Simon Ark, who claims to be over a thousand years old and says of himself, "I make a hobby of investigating any strange or unexplained happenings in the world ... I am searching for the ultimate evil - for Satan himself." In "Village of the Dead" (*Famous Detective Stories* Dec. 1955), Ark appears in the Western town of Gidaz where, in a powerful beginning, we learn that the entire population has committed suicide by walking off the edge of a cliff. (This was 23 years before the mass suicide in Jonestown.) The deaths are related to a religious group, a branch of the Danatist schism which split away from the Roman Catholic church in the 4th century and believed in martyrdom. Ark, whose solutions are always realistic, was perfect for mysteries about religious cults and one of the best in the series is "The Vicar of Hell" (*Famous Detective Stories* Aug. 1956), involving the search for the only extant copy of a book called "The Worship of Satan," supposed to include the forbidden rituals of devil worship. The book is tied to two 16th century murders and now is the apparent cause of another, in 20th century London, with the victim crucified by arrows in a room in a pub where Black Masses take place.

In "Sword for a Sinner" (*Saint Mystery Magazine* Oct. 1959; reprinted in *The Judges of Hades*, 1971), Hoch involves Simon Ark with a bizarre religious sect which actually existed in the United States. The Penitentes, an offshoot of Roman Catholicism found primarily in isolated portions of New Mexico, engaged in practices of self-flagellation which led to their being banned by the church in the 19th century.

Rumors of their continued existence have persisted. A popular 1930s exploitation film was titled *Lash of the Pentitentes*. As recently as 1990 the author of this article heard rumors of their continued existence in the mountains of Northern New Mexico. In the Hoch story this "illegal" sect is alive, if not well, in the Sangre de Cristo Mountains, north of Santa Fe. Ark investigates murder among the Brotherhood of the Penitentes, a group whose members are tied to crosses, in emulation of Jesus Christ. They are introduced to the reader in properly dramatic fashion by Hoch's narrator, "In that moment I thought

I'd stepped into a madhouse, but there was worse to come."

More than thirty years (and over 700 stories) after his debut, Hoch dealt with a different type of cult in "The Way up to Hades" (*Alfred Hitchcock's Mystery Magazine* Jan. 1988). Ark attends a rock concert at Madison Square Garden because a popular singer, Rager, claims to summon the devil during his performances. (The singer's cynical manager says, however, "No one believes in Satan any more. He's got even less of a following than God.") True to Hochian form, there is an impossible crime and also a story which emphasizes that to many young people today rock music and its idols have inspired a form of cult worship.

Francis M. Nevins' *The Ninety-Million-Dollar Mouse* (1987) was written before the PTL and Swaggart scandals broke, thereby making it all the more remarkable. Drakeism is a "religion" with its own university, television and radio stations, amusement park, and publishing company. Many of the ways in which the Drakeans collect money are reminiscent of television evangelism. The book contains an episode in which a church leader forces a woman to have sex with him. Unfortunately, it is never quite believable why so many people would have been "converted," because Drakeism, unlike the PTL, for example, does not rely on Christianity. It seems like mumbo-jumbo, mostly centering around its basic symbol of the egg, though that may be part of Nevins' thesis about *all* religions. There is something especially fitting about Nevins setting his con man, Milo Turner, to defeat a con religion.

Other mysteries, if not anticipatory, reflected their times. Ivor Drummond's *The Priests of the Abomination* (1970) combines the movement to end the war in Vietnam with the sexual revolution and provides a Southern California church which offers both. One of their gurus, Miranda, an Englishwoman of perverted sexual tastes, leads members in an orgy, telling them that this was what God liked. They are joined by a British bishop who is very trendy and has been called "The Beat Bishop ... the Swinging Sermoniser ... The Padre of the Protest Marches." Drummond has his group use the media in ways that Anthony Boucher might never have thought of, had he not been so good a science fiction writer too. "Every trick of showmanship and communications was invoked ... borrowed from the Roman and Greek churches ... and the religions of the East ... tall candles glowing out of velvety blackness, incantatory voices from high dark pulpits, sudden gigantic crashes of organ music, invisible choirs...."

An alumni of the peace movement is Roger L. Simon's Moses Wine in *The Big Fix* (1973). Wine is "a dropped-out, debt-ridden, divorced, dope-smoking dick" in Southern California who gets hired to find out how flyers linking a Presidential hopeful to a radical political group are being circulated. Along the way he comes across the Human Potential Movement, led by Swami Sri Prasanamurti, and the Church of the Five Deities, two religious groups which have political connections. He also visits Barney's Voodoo Store on Hollywood Boulevard where they offer to sell him The Pentagram of Solomon, which wards off evil spirits, or "exclusive Satan cocktail napkins with the inverted cross, at $7.50 the dozen. A great conversation stimulus." He meets a woman who tells him that "A few years ago Satanism was all the rage. Then along came Esalen with encounter groups, nude therapy. People were mixed up. Misled. They didn't realize the Devil was more than just another kookie Southern California fad." She complains that Charles Manson was a phony who gave satanists a bad name.

One of Manson's disciples attempted to

assassinate President Gerald Ford in 1976, the year Woody Allen published "Nefarious Times We Live In." Allen's "hero," Willard Pogrebin, is en route to Hollywood when he is picked up by members of a cult. "I recall being driven to a deserted ranch where several mesmerized young women force fed me organic health foods and then tried to emboss the sign of the pentagram on my forehead with a soldering iron. I then witnessed a black mass in which hooded adolescent acolytes chanted the words, 'Oh wow,' in Latin."

Later Pogrebin is "solicited by ardent proselytizers on the street to seek religious salvation with The Reverend Chow Bok Ding, a moon-faced charismatic ... an esthetic man who renounced all worldly possessions in excess of those owned by Charles Foster Kane." Eventually, in this very funny short story, Pogrebin becomes involved in a presidential assassination attempt.

Children, flower and otherwise, are often the object of California cults, and several mysteries dealt with this more seriously than did Allen. Thomas B. Dewey's Mac is in Los Angeles to find a missing 17-year-old girl in *The Love-Death Thing* (1969). He meets a character called the Prophet Daniel who sells underground newspapers with "Complete directions how to save the world. Your last chance." Displaying his usual empathy for the young, Mac battles rackets that would take advantage of them, as well as that other Southern California staple, a biker group like the Hell's Angels.

The basic elements found in Dewey are present in Arthur Lyons' *All God's Children* (1975), but the book is far from a copy. Los Angeles private eye Jacob Asch is hired to find Susan Gurney, daughter of wealthy parents, who had run off before her high school finals to join the Word of God. Her parents had her brought back (actually kidnapped) by a professional deprogrammer, but now she has run off again, probably back to the cult, though she is also involved with Gypsy, a member of a biker gang called Satan's Warriors.

In one of the best scenes in the book, Asch goes to Hollywood Boulevard to see how the cult picks up recruits. He watches them approaching young, vulnerable runaway kids, offering them a free meal and taking them by bus to the remote Santa Paula Valley. (They make sure there is no transportation readily available for those who choose not to stay.) The group's leader is a former used car salesman who now calls himself "Moses." One of his first converts was an ex-Green Beret, now known as Brother Isaiah, who has organized the group along military lines, imposing rigid discipline, while forcing recruits to farm the commune's agricultural fields. Asch enters their compound and, after a few sarcastic comments, he is accused of being an atheist. He replies, quoting Somerset Maugham, "I find it very difficult to believe in a God less tolerant than I am." He soon finds that he needs more than mere wisecracks to combat this group.

When William Campbell Gault published *The Dead Seed* (1985), the idea of religious cults attracting the young, even in Southern California, seemed oddly dated, so fast does our society change. He has a group called The New Awareness, but gives little description of them, except that they force their members to make pottery and rugs and sell them on the beaches. He includes a crooked deprogrammer who splits his fees with the cult leader. The cult, like the book, is surprisingly dull.

In *The First Detective* (1984) Joseph McNamara, Chief of Police of San Jose, California, demonstrates that religious cults have permeated the "Silicon Valley" too. The police are looking for a missing 16-year-old girl who may have been taken by The Moral Reaffirmation Guild, a commune whose slogan is "self awareness through moral reaffirmation," but who really use young children as sexual objects for the Hollywood and Las Vegas "kiddy porno" market and also to blackmail political figures. Drawing analogies to Jonestown, Vietnamese prison camps, the Krishnas, the Moonies et al, one character says,

> They were conditioning those youngsters. You know the formula: long sessions of silence, no sleep, little food, then constant chanting. They were taught to sit staring into each other's eyes for hours without speaking or moving. A standard disorientation technique.... Gradually people perform as directed. Emotion and feelings vanish, along with anything resembling formerly held value systems.

McNamara alludes to the difficulties in combatting these groups because their activities have often been construed by the courts as religious and protected by the First Amendment.

"California has become a sanctuary for the psychic refuse of the world," says a physician whose attempts to treat a small boy suffering from cancer may be thwarted by the influence over his parents of a religious group called "The Touch" in Jonathan Kellerman's *Blood Test* (1986). The psychiatric social worker on the case describes two members as having "that glazed look in their eyes—the I-know-the-secret-of-the-universe-but-I-won't-tell-you trance. Moonies, Krishnas, Esties, Touchers, they're all the same." The Touch is a group of about sixty, mostly middle-aged, which is not looking for converts. "In practical terms that means you don't have parents screaming to the cops or calling in the deprogrammers."

Looking for the child, Kellerman's series character, psychologist Alex Delaware, goes to their base, "The Retreat," a converted Catholic monastery near the Mexican border. There he finds the cult's leader, now calling himself Noble Matthias, once a successful Beverly Hills attorney who was known as "shyster to the stars." Matthias was shot in the head by an irate client's husband, after which he achieved "sanctification through brain damage." In describing his group's philosophy, Noble says, "We are refugees from a former life. We've chosen a new life that emphasizes purity and industry." Delaware is rightly skeptical, saying, "Standard stuff. He rattled it off like some New Age pledge of allegiance." Later, observing some members sitting yoga-style on the grass, he finds that "despite the white costumes, the sandals, and the untrimmed beards, they resembled participants in a corporate seminar, one of those glossy pop-psych affairs promoted by management to increase productivity." The group shows its true colors when Delaware sees them in a cocaine-sniffing, sexual orgy which Kellerman describes in far more detail than is necessary unless his purpose is shock or titillation. Writing about child abuse, McNamara and Kellerman, if somewhat trendy, dealt with powerful and very affecting subject matter.

The relationship between political extremism and religious cults was not merely the province of writers like Wheatley. Even John D. MacDonald made the connection with *The Green Ripper* (1979), probably his most powerful novel. MacDonald sends Travis McGee, with believable motivation, on a personal mission to infiltrate the Church of the Apocrypha in California. Before finding it he is told by someone living nearby,

> 'Friend, this state is chock-full of religions. You can find any kind you are

looking for. There's some that'll take you to Guyana and teach you to raise oranges and how to kill yourself quick. They start in the north and go all the way down to the Mexican border, and to my way of thinking, the further south they go, the crazier they get. People are hunting around for something to believe in these days. All the stuff people used to believe in has kind of let them down hard.'

McGee finds the terrorist arm of the cult, its main reason for being, run by fanatics who are training to wreak havoc throughout the United States. They wish to change the world and operate under the idea that

> A true zealot can be a fearsome engine of destruction....The most bloody, savage, awful acts that seem the most pointless, they're the ones that are most productive. They revolt and shock everyone, and that puts terrible pressure on the central government and local governments to crack down on *all* the people who are nonconformist in any way. When that happens, the resentment makes rebels out of the conformists too, and pretty soon the whole structure crumbles.

A book that is moving and exciting throughout is capped by one of the most exciting climaxes in the entire John D. MacDonald canon.

While researching and writing this article, I found myself continuously coming across articles in the newspapers about abuses under the name of religion, many of which involved cults. There is no reason to believe this trend will not continue, thus providing, since art imitates life (and vice versa), much material for the mystery writers of the future.

MORMON MYSTERIES

by Jon L. Breen

The Church of Jesus Christ of Latter-Day Saints has not enjoyed a good press in mystery fiction. There is no Mormon equivalent of Father Brown or Rabbi Small or Reverend Randollph to represent the tenets of the faith in the course of detecting crime. And whatever the fine attributes of the church, it has most often appeared in as menacing a fictional guise as the KGB.

Arthur Conan Doyle's *A Study in Scarlet* (1887), the first Sherlock Holmes novel, may or may not have also been the first detective novel with considerable Mormon content, but it is clearly the only one from the Nineteenth Century that has remained continuously in print. And to a Mormon Sherlockian, it must be the same sort of embarrassment that D.W. Griffith's *Birth of a Nation* is to a film scholar: important as a pioneering masterpiece of its form, but distasteful at best and dangerous at worst in the attitude it conveys to a particular group of people (blacks, in the case of the Griffith film).

The first part of *A Study in Scarlet*, narrated by Dr. Watson, describes his first meeting with Sherlock Holmes and the consulting detective's investigation of a murder at 3 Lauriston Gardens. The victim is Enoch J. Drebber, a visiting American from Cleveland, Ohio. His supposed secretary, Joseph Stangerson, also becomes a murder victim, and slightly past the halfway mark of the novel, Holmes is able to pin the crime on cabman Jefferson Hope. The second part, "The Country of the Saints," uses about 35% of the short novel's total wordage to explain the motive for the crimes. Despite its reputation for dullness, the Mormon section of *Scarlet* is a good if florid piece of storytelling—Conan Doyle's narrative gifts didn't desert him when he wasn't writing about Holmes and Watson—but western adventure is not what the Holmes reader is commonly looking for.

A band of almost 10,000 Mormons are crossing the Great Alkali Plain when they come upon John Ferris and five-year-old Lucy, last survivors of an ill-fated party. The rescuers identify themselves as "the persecuted children of God—the chosen of the Angel Merona [sic]," fleeing their previous settlement in Nauvoo, Illinois, "to seek a refuge from the violent man and the godless, even though in the heart of the desert." Prophet Brigham Young allows the Ferrises to join the caravan on the condition they adopt the Mormon faith. Care of the newcomers is assigned to Elder Stangerson. Another of the four principal elders is named Drebber.

John Ferris follows the faith in most of its aspects and becomes one of the wealthiest men in Salt Lake City, but he remains celibate, refusing to set up a polygamous household. Lucy is courted by a Gentile named Jefferson Hope, and Ferris is determined that she never marry a Mormon, such being "no marriage at all ... a shame and a disgrace." He keeps his feelings quiet, however, because "to express an unorthodox opinion was a dangerous matter in those days in the Land of the Saints." In fact, Doyle tells us, "The victims of persecution had now turned persecutors on their own account," comparable to the Spanish Inquisition and "the secret societies of Italy." It is rumored that the Danite Band, or Avenging Angels, raid non-Mormon camps to increase the supply of available women for purposes of polygamy, which "without a female population on which to draw was a barren doctrine indeed."

Brigham Young himself visits Ferris, both to urge him into polygamy and warn him not to let Lucy wed a Gentile. Young says she must choose between sons of Drebber and Stangerson and gives Ferris a one-month deadline for her decision. The two men visit to present their cases: Stangerson, having a mere four wives to Drebber's seven, believes he has the stronger claim, but Drebber counters that he is wealthier. Ferris runs them both off his property.

With time running out, Hope helps the Ferrises to flee. However, while he is away hunting, a Mormon party overtakes the Ferrises, killing him and returning her for purposes of marriage. Returning to the city, Hope learns Lucy has been married to Drebber but "pined away and died within a month." Hope appears at the bier and snatches the wedding ring from her finger. Attempts on the lives of Drebber and Stangerson fail. Returning after an absence (presumably caused by the Civil War), Hope discovers the pair have left the church in a schism with the elders and left for parts unknown. Hope finally tracks them down in England.

In his monograph *Conan Doyle and the Latter-Day Saints*, Sherlockian scholar Jack Tracy, observing the irregular convention that Watson was the author of the Holmes adventures and Doyle the agent, theorizes that "The Country of the Saints" was written by Doyle himself in order to fill out the story to novel length. Tracy sees the story as a part of the wave of anti-Mormon literature current in the 1880s, most of it forgotten while *A Study in Scarlet*, because of its significance as a classic of detective fiction, remains continuously available. His goal is "to refute the slanders on the Latter-Day Saints which so greatly mar our introduction to the career of Sherlock Holmes" (page 14). Certainly, he exposes factual errors in Doyle's narrative, including the inflated number of

10,000 in the rescue party and Brigham Young's age at the time of the incident. He states the insistence that the Ferrises convert to be rescued is contrary to "the Mormons' often-demonstrated generosity toward their fellow travellers" (page 24). The depiction of Young's "heartless fanaticism ... slanders a great and compassionate man" (page 24). Tracy states the Mountain Meadow Massacre, an isolated incident, was responsible for the rumors of Mormon attacks on wagon trains.

Tracy concludes that *Scarlet*'s "Mormon interlude" is "entirely fictitious" (page 67), though presumably Watson's account is not, and recounts Doyle's good reception in Utah in 1922 (when there to lecture on spiritualism) and his changed attitude toward the Latter-Day Saints.

The better part of a century passed before more detective fiction with strong Mormon content was to appear, and again the picture of the church was largely a negative one. This recent wave of mystery fiction with a Mormon background began with three 1983 novels.

Rex Burns' *The Avenging Angel* (Viking) involves Denver cop Gabe Wager with a series of murders involving Mormon fundamentalists, i.e. those who have continued to practice polygamy in defiance of the church's revelation against it in the 1880s. The first victim, found shot to death on a road east of Denver, has in his hand a drawing of an angel with a sword. Soon a connection is made with the Danites, the Avenging Angels of the title. Wager visits Grant County, Colorado, a hotbed of fundamentalism. Local editor Orrin Winston, a self-described jack-Mormon, is a product of polygamy though he doesn't believe in it himself. He tells Wager the revelation against the practice was a political rather than a religious event. Sheriff Tice, who turns a blind eye to the fundamentalists because their votes keep him in office, tells Wager the "hard-shelled, unreformed Mormons" believe "Negroes are Satan's children ... Indians are red because they broke God's commandments ... polygamy's still one of God's laws" (page 41). The novel is highly readable and entertaining, marked by the author's railing against contemporary society in the John D. MacDonald manner, but the case is strictly a battle of offshoots, with no involvement (and thus no indictment) of the L.D.S. Church proper.

Thomas H. Cook's *Tabernacle* (Houghton Mifflin) presents a familiar (in fact, over-familiar) situation in crime fiction of the 1980s: big-city cop hunts crazy serial killer. The difference is that Detective Tom Jackson, a former New York cop and a non-Mormon, doesn't know right away that the perpetrator of a series of Salt Lake City murders is the same person, so various are the weapons used and the stations in life of the victims: a strangled black prostitute, a shot Mormon reporter, a stabbed official of the church's Public Communications Department, a young Brigham Young University coed who witnessed the latter's death, and finally a church archivist (again shot) and his two sons. The reader knows they are connected, however; that each victim is seen by the anonymous killer as despoiling his clean dream of the Saints.

The plot is superbly worked out, but the use of the Salt Lake locale is one of the novel's strongest points. Jackson and the other "non-Mormons who lived in Salt Lake formed a kind of secret brotherhood of the damned. They floated in the bloodstream of the city like foreign objects, but they had nothing to hold them together except their shared isolation from the pervasive Mormon atmosphere" (page 12). Sometimes, says a non-Mormon waitress, "You feel like a fly in a prayer book. The weight of Salt Lake just comes slamming down on you" (page 15).

Gary Stewart's *The Tenth Virgin* (St. Martin's) is the first Mormon mystery to my knowledge actually written by a Mormon. According to the jacket copy, Stewart, a theatre professor at Indiana State University, Terre Haute, "was born in Salt Lake City and ... grew up assuming that most of the civilized world was Mormon, that most everybody had horses, that it was common to have a multitude of great-grandmothers, and that just about everybody had relatives living in polygamous communes." His detective, New York private eye and lapsed Mormon Gabe Utley, returns to Salt Lake City to take a case for an old friend. In his hotel room, he watches an L.D.S. apostle lecturing about family values on TV. "I turned off the set when I started feeling guilty about my recent divorce" (page 3). Client Linda Young Peterson wants Gabe to find her missing daughter Jennifer, who she fears may have been kidnapped by fundamentalists. David, the girl's father, doesn't know she's gone and mustn't be involved lest his position in the church hierarchy be endangered.

If you want to avoid a partial revelation of the ending, skip this paragraph. The solution reveals a double agent, a member of the Twelve Apostles who is also the prophet of a fundamentalist sect. He uses his position to help fundamentalists sneak into the Temple for marriage ceremonies. Gabe is reminded "the major thing the Mormon Church has that the Fundamentalist sects don't have—besides several billion dollars and respectability—is access to the Temple" (page 240).

In the second book in the series, *The Zarahemla Vision* (St. Martin's, 1986), we find Utley has stayed on to become a full-fledged Salt Lake private eye. "What a way to make a living. But you can't beat an uptight religious society for providing employment for parasites such as me. These Mormons take their adultery seriously" (page 9).

Gabe learns from his Aunt Hattie that cousin Parley claims to have kidnapped the President of the Mormon Church. Parley says he has been helped by an angel who may be one of the Three Nephites—North American apostles Christ allowed to live until his Second Coming, they wander the earth and do good deeds. Meanwhile, the Mormon President is reported to have died in his sleep in the penthouse suite of the Hotel Utah.

The plot concerns the treatment of Native Americans by the Mormon Church. In the Book of Mormon, Indians are called Laminites—they are eligible to be made "white and delightsome" as full-fledged Mormons. The Indian Placement Service, started in the 1930s, places Indians to live with Mormon families, thereby spawning a people lost between two cultures. Thomas Running Bear takes the titular "Zarahelma" file from the prophet's quarters—he is subsequently murdered and the file stolen.

In this second book, the detective (and implicitly the author) seem ambivalent toward Mormonism. They see its hypocrisies and inconsistencies but also admire its pioneers and traditions. Early in the novel, we learn Utley still considers himself a Mormon. "You don't shake that off like honeybees" (page 47). Near the end, he states that he is "Mormon to my bone" (page 253) and argues that non-observant Mormons stay *cultural* Mormons, in the same sense as cultural Jews or Catholics.

Were it not for the Mormon content, the two Utley books would be very routine private eye novels. They tend to be a bit padded and overlong, and they lean on such plot clichés as anonymous warnings and blows to the head. Despite many local details, the Salt Lake background is not captured with any special spark or flavor. Utley and the continuing secondary characters have their moments—Alvin Smith IV, the

Prophet's nephew and Assistant Director for Church Public Communications, is especially promising in the first book, and Irish-Chicana *Deseret News* reporter Mona McKinley makes an okay Susan Silverman character—but they lack the vitality of figures that support long series.

Still, though each book is centered on an unpleasant aspect of the L.D.S. religion—polygamy in the first, racism toward Native Americans in the second—the Utley novels come the closest to being detective fiction written from inside the church. With the spectre of the last scene of the second book in mind—Utley opting for apricot nectar instead of bourbon—the reader is left curious as to what the third book in the series will be like.

Cleo Jones' *Prophet Motive* (St. Martin's, 1984) is the work of an ex-Mormon living in Berkeley, California, who also wrote the novel *Sister Wives* about the family of Brigham Young. It is a strongly feminist novel, written from a believably *masculine* viewpoint—not a bad trick at all.

A third-person prologue finds young Timothy Dade struggling against seduction by Sarah Manion, the bishop's daughter. Before anything can happen, they find her father's body in the snow, killed by a butcher knife. We then meet narrator Christopher Danville, lapsed Mormon and police chief of Magpie, Utah, investigating his first murder. Magpie is a growing "bedroom community for Salt Lake" (page 10), about twenty miles south of the city. It has twenty wards, and thus twenty bishops.

Danville identifies two types of Mormons, Iron Rod Saints and Liahonas:

> In a Book of Mormon vision an iron rod ran straight through the fog of

ignorance and error to the tree of life. Iron Rod Saints kept their hands on that rod, kept to the straight path, kept the word. They tithed conscientiously, never used birth control, didn't smoke, didn't drink booze, tea, coffee, or Coke, and condemned those that did. I've heard it said some Iron Rods will ask a blessing over a bag of Planter's peanuts. The Liahona was a Book of Mormon compass. Liahona Saints just generally moved in the right direction—more or less (page 12).

Fingered as a suspect in the murder is Naomi Green ("one of those libbers," page 14), who supported the Magpie Planned Parenthood offices and had battled the bishop. She had helped his wife get fitted with a diaphragm and (per the prologue) also given birth control advice to the bishop's daughter. Footprints in the snow lead to her house. Another suspect is Danville's sergeant, Preston Wilks, whom he discovers to be a closet fundamentalist, believing himself the "One Mighty and Strong," the last Prophet before the Millennium.

The only Mormon mystery to my knowledge written by a woman, *Prophet Motive* has as its theme the oppression of women in the L.D.S. church. This emphasis produces much information on Mormon sexual mores and taboos. Boys are told "no touching" (i.e. masturbation), but no one would bother to tell this to the girls "since innocent womanhood wouldn't do that" (page 22). Interviewing Naomi Green, Danville counters "the popular conception of polygamy" as lust: "Fundamentalists never approach their wives unless the lady expresses a wish for another child" (page 45).

"Food," Danville reports, "is the one permissible Mormon vice, and most of our women tend to be overweight. The Prophet declared once that being overweight, too, was against the word of wisdom, and the next day thousands of women hit the streets all dressed in pink jogging suits" (page 59).

The chief's description of a Mormon woman's kitchen also speaks volumes: "Counted cross-stitch slogans on the walls, the toaster covered with a gingham chicken, the blender with a calico doll, and the dish detergent bottle with a little ruffled apron. I don't think there's a naked dish detergent bottle in the whole state of Utah" (page 61).

Aside from matters of sexual politics, Jones makes many pointed observations about the power of the Mormon church—members of church security "by a special act of the Utah Legislature, have full police powers anywhere in the state" (page 151)—and its odd inconsistencies: "though Saints aren't allowed to gamble, they are allowed to own casinos" (page 69). She (via narrator Danville) observes about the church's most serious public relations problem of recent years, "a number of those who demonstrated to get priesthood status for blacks were excommunicated and not reinstated when black priesthood was granted. It was ironic—blacks can now gain the highest degree of heaven, but those who spoke for them are forever doomed to the lower floors, the celestial back of the bus" (page 67).

Prophet Motive is more steeped in Mormon doctrine and social mores than any other Mormon mystery novel, at least partly because it is essentially a small-town mystery rather than being based in Salt Lake City. As would be expected in the work of a feminist ex-Mormon, it is also the angriest of the books in its view of the church and its hypocrisies. That anger spills out in a very moving and effective final scene.

The most recent Mormon mystery novels, and

among the best, are the first three cases for Moroni Traveler, Salt Lake City private eye. Like his creator, Robert Irvine, Traveler is a non-Mormon who grew up in Salt Lake. *Baptism for the Dead* (Dodd, Mead, 1988) opens with Penny Snow asking Traveler to find her mother, Martha Varney, driven away six years before by her father, a member of the Council of Seventy. The title refers to the Mormon practice of baptizing their ancestors by proxy, a principal reason for the Mormon obsession with genealogy. Before turning away from the church in disgust, Penny had begged her father to have her mother baptized in absentia, a course he declined in the absence of proof she was dead.

Irvine introduces a number of characters who will recur in future books in the series. Mad Bill is a street preacher who carries a sign admonishing the citizens to repent while there's still time. Willis Tanner is a boyhood friend, now a Mormon church public relations trouble-shooter with whom Traveler maintains as much of a friendship as a "gentile" can with a Saint as well as an occasional professional relationship—Tanner constantly hopes to convert Traveler to the one true church, claiming the private eye must have been named Moroni, after the official Mormon angel, for a reason. Traveler's father, Martin, is his professional mentor and a sometime partner in his investigations. Claire Benyon is a former girlfriend who is always calling on Traveler to bail her out of trouble—and though the troubles are often imaginary, he always does.

Tanner tells Traveler that Martha Varney ran away to join a fundamentalist cult called the Church of Zion Reborn. A member of the cult, Earl Jordan, was recently murdered. Tanner wants to hire Traveler to represent the church's interests, working to discredit the cult while protecting the Varneys from publicity in connection with Jordan's death. Traveler is told the prophet, Elton Wooley, is taking a personal interest in the case. Cooperating can bring Traveler plenty of the church's investigation business. The story, involving like some real-life Mormon mysteries an inflammatory church document, moves swiftly and economically while getting into the skins of its characters and making effective use of the Salt Lake background.

The second book in the series, *The Angels' Share* (St. Martin's, 1989), fulfills the promise of the first, exploring Traveler's relationship with the other continuing characters in greater depth. As the story opens, Irvine makes the reader feel the 100-degree July heat and whiff the "rotten-egg smell of the Great Salt Lake" (page 2). It is four days to Pioneer Day (July 24), which commemorates the anniversary of the Mormons' first arrival in Salt Lake. Traveler's clients are Newell Farnsworth, a bishop and dentist, and daughter Suzanne, whose fiancé Heber Armstrong had disappeared in England just a month before he was due to come home from his mission. But Suzanne saw him in Salt Lake only two days before. Traveler takes the assignment to find him. Privately, Suzanne tells him Armstrong had written her "he wasn't coming back. He said he'd lost his faith and called himself a missionary of the damned" (page 9).

The elegant Hotel Utah has been converted into a Mormon office building where Willis Tanner is headquartered. Tanner tries to warn Traveler off the case, which is "church business pure and simple" (page 31). Later, however, he once again has Traveler in the church's employ, to find a Ripper-like Salt Lake serial killer who produces his own promotional video, ending with the menacing words, "Jack's back" (page 144). The theory is that the killer, who quotes the Book of Mormon, may be a missionary-gone-astray with TV training. The third victim has a sheet of paper in her vagina saying "the angels' share" (page 150). Tanner tells Traveler,

> In 1840 Joseph Smith himself sent Brigham Young on a mission to England. We were a poor lot in those days. The poor can't pay a tithe when they have nothing. Brigham knew that. Tradition says that he came up with a solution. I'll pay my tithe in converts. That will be my angels' share (page 151).

Martin Traveler becomes a more prominent character in the second book. Suffering from a tumor in his throat, the elder heretic begins to hedge his bets religiously, even turning in desperation to faith-healer Orson Pack. Pack belongs to an offshoot group called Saints of the Last Day who do not believe in sex or children. They wear trousers buttoned in back. "The fly in front," says Pack, "came into fashion for only one reason, to create fornication pants, as Brigham Young called them" (page 107).

The Traveler series, like much contemporary detective fiction, places an emphasis on looking back and reassessing earlier events in the protagonist's life. In the third book, *Gone to Glory* (St. Martin's, 1990), Traveler looks into the case of a boyhood hero, minor league shortstop Pepper Dalton, who has been accused of the murder of his sister over sale of the old mining town of Glory, which they have inherited. Pepper wants to sell the property to finance buying the Salt Lake City baseball team, which he wants to restore to its former stature, while she wants to keep it for her polygamous husband Zeke Eldredge. Suspect Dalton is off-stage through most of the novel, leading the reader to wonder what kind of a guy Traveler's old hero really is. As he often does, Irvine provides a satisfactory final twist separate from the main mystery.

Traveler's relationship with his father, Martin, his

troublesome girlfriend, Claire, and his boyhood friend Willis Tanner continue to develop in interesting ways, and there are new details of Mormon folkways. A tobacco-chewing ballplayer comments on the church's attitude toward his habit:

> 'There's no distinction around here. You never know when a sin's going to get you arrested. Or what qualifies as a sin either, for that matter.... Take tobacco, for instance. Joe Smith and Brigham Young chewed it themselves in the beginning, you know. It was Smith's wife who put a stop to it. She got tired of him and his friends spitting on her floor. So she kept after him until he had a revelation' (page 122).

Irvine's three novels are the most promising series of Mormon mysteries. The reader has the impression there is an infinite amount of material still to be explored, both in the characters and in the ins and outs of the L.D.S. religion.

In my opinion, the Mormon mystery novels hit for a higher average strictly in terms of quality than their Catholic and Protestant brethren. This will be no comfort to the Mormon mystery reader, however. The stories stress the criminous and/or absurd aspects of the religion, with nothing from within the Mormon church itself to balance them.

Will there ever be a L.D.S. Father Brown? Will there ever be Mormon detective stories written by an apologist for the religion rather than by a skeptic? It is doubtful. While some Mormon scholars are committed to investigation of its roots, thereby sometimes endangering their status in the church, the religion as a whole puts much more emphasis on obedience. Religions whose primary documents go back thousands of years can afford to tolerate (even encourage) inquiring minds in a way a religion barely 150 years old cannot.

RELIGIOUS DETECTIVE FICTION:
A SYMPOSIUM OF PRACTITIONERS

by Ellis Peters, William X. Kienzle, Harry Kemelman and Sister Carol Anne O'Marie

Several authors of mystery novels about religious detectives were asked to respond to a group of questions. Responding to the questions individually were Ellis Peters and William X. Kienzle. Their replies follow.

> 1) What are the main advantages and disadvantages of using a member of the clergy or a member of a religious order as a continuing detective?

PETERS: One advantage is that his approach must rest mainly on observation of character, which interests me far more than forensic detail. Especially is this true if the books are set in the twelfth century. Another advantage is that the genuine effort to create such a protagonist obliges, rather than allows, you to put into his mouth things you may profoundly believe, but which would come very oddly from a different type of person. Sometimes you even end enlightening and convincing yourself!

KIENZLE: Advantages: I've found it a natural way to create a series using the same celibate sleuth (eleven books to date). Having the clergy around tends to create a genteel atmosphere. It is an almost inevitable way of introducing interesting moral concepts, dilemmas, etc. No disadvantages come to mind.

2) How does your religious viewpoint influence your choice of victims and murderers?

PETERS: They're all human beings. Sometimes the gap between victim and murderer is very small indeed. Someone who cares about individual souls can't discard either the murderer or the victim. I admit the early church and many of the legendary saints in particular were chiefly notable for their ferocity towards anyone who crossed them, but the priests and brothers who had parochial cares had to rub shoulders with all sorts and conditions of men. I see few I would call villains.

KIENZLE: I tend to think in terms of virtue and vice. More often than not, my victims represent vice. If I can help it, I don't want to pick on virtue. So, certifiable sleazeballs are more likely to get it. My murderers tend to be complex characters with some reasons for what they do.

3) How (if at all) have your writings in the detective fiction field altered or developed your own religious views and attitudes?

PETERS: Brother Cadfael is a very comfortable influence in my own life. The effort to make him real has enabled him to talk back to me. My beliefs have not changed, but they have been reinforced.

KIENZLE: I grew to believe that morality usually travels in shades of gray and hardly ever in strict blacks and whites. My experience in writing about virtue and vice has reinforced the above concept.

4) What effect would you like your writings to have on your readers' religious views? Can detective fiction be used as a vehicle for gaining converts?

PETERS: I'm not aiming to convert anyone, but I would like my books to make people feel better, not worse, about being human, and more optimistic about being able to push on and improve, somewhere, on what we are here.

KIENZLE: I have a letter from a woman in New York who confesses being a lapsed Catholic. As a result of reading my books, she wrote she was amazed at all the interesting things going on in the Catholic Church. She promised to go back to church and find out for herself. Also, faithful readers of my books would have all the information necessary to grant oneself a do-it-yourself declaration of nullity of marriage—if such were needed.

5) Why have Roman Catholic religious detectives so far outnumbered Jewish and Protestant religious detectives?

PETERS: I suppose that the Christian Church was one for so long that the Catholic part of it remains the stem. I am not Catholic myself, but of course in Cadfael's day we all were—or pagans—and the faith at that time was relatively simple and pure, compared with the schisms and disputes of later centuries. Perhaps, also, the figure of the priest in the Catholic Church has a much more authoritative and dominant role than in most Protestant faiths, so that he ranks high as a possible protagonist in any battle with evil.

KIENZLE: The subject is mystery novels. I believe the nature of the priesthood (a macho, asexual, celibate man) is in itself a mystery to the non-priest, Catholic and non-Catholic alike. Also, most fictional detectives are unmarried. Sifting through clues and red herrings works better when the sleuth is unencumbered by emotional encumbrances. Priests are not only celibate, they are also, or should be (mine are) alone to figure things out themselves.

6) What other writer(s) of religious detective fiction (historical or contemporary) do you most admire, and why?

PETERS: Father Brown is the most obvious candidate, hard to resist because of the brilliance of his use of paradox, a kind of updated spiritual dialectic close kin to the methods of the scholastics of about the eleventh and twelfth centuries.

KIENZLE: The creator of the "Father Dowling" series, Ralph McInerny. He is one of only two writers with whom I am familiar who, although they never were priests, seem to know what is like being a priest. The other is J.F. Powers.

Two other writers chose to respond with an individual statement. First, Harry Kemelman, author of the Rabbi Small books:

My use of the rabbi as a detective is purely accidental. I had written a book about the building of a new temple and my editor objected to it on the grounds that it was too low-keyed. He suggested jokingly that it might liven it up if I were to get some of the Nicky Welt business into it. On my way home, I passed the local temple and it occurred to me that the large parking lot in front of it would be a good place to deposit a body. That's how I happened to write *Friday, the Rabbi Slept Late*. Since Nicky Welt's reasoning was essentially Talmudic, there was no problem.

The purpose of the books is to teach and explain Judaism to Jews and Gentiles. The fact that the books, particularly *Conversations with Rabbi Small* are used in theology schools, seminaries, and conversion classes, indicates, I think, that they appear to serve their purpose.

(Editor's Note: The Nicky Welt referred to is the detective in a series of short stories Kemelman wrote for *Ellery Queen's Mystery Magazine*, beginning with the classic "The Nine-Mile Walk." The stories were collected under that title in a 1967 volume. *Conversations with Rabbi Small* is a non-mystery volume in which the Rabbi advises a young woman who wants to convert to her fiance's religion of Judaism.)

And finally Sister Carol Anne O'Marie, in an essay which appeared in an earlier version in *The Mystery Readers of America Journal*, Spring 1987:

A HABIT FOR MURDER

by Sister Carol Anne O'Marie

Picking a religious as a series sleuth, especially if that religious happens to be a nun is, to my mind, like picking a winner. Why? Because nuns are inherently mysterious. Furthermore, there seems to be a universal fascination with them. If fascination is too strong a word, most people are, at least, curious about them.

And if you think about it, you can understand why. For centuries, these serene-faced women were swathed in long, flowing habits. The combination of starched, white linen and black serge hid or, at least, changed their appearances.

Then there is the matter of their names. Many use only first names; names like Sister Petronilla or Ladislaus or Eutichiana. Even the most trusting of us suspects that no mother in her right mind, since Roman times, anyway, would christen her infant daughter "Petronilla." So, we conclude, these are not their real names. These are "religious" names. Which sets us wondering about these women who conceal both their appearances and their family names. Who are they *really* and what are they trying to hide?

Are you beginning to see my point about picking a winner? And I'm not finished yet. There is the tantalizing business of the rules of the cloister. What is buried beyond those dim, hushed, antiseptically clean hallways? Why is no one allowed inside except other nuns, of course, and an occasional priest? Why do they keep real people out? Or is it that they (whoever "they" may be) are trying to keep the nuns inside? To an active imagination, it is all very baffling and mysterious, perhaps even sinister.

Moreover, many people, even those who should know better, consider nuns to be meek, sheltered, ineffectual creatures removed completely from evil. What does a nun know, they reason, of greed, or envy, or loathing? They imagine that these women, shrouded and cloistered as they are, must be unfamiliar with all emotions, but especially unaware of those base emotions which lead to murder. Sister is shockingly out of place in a murder mystery. An excellent reason, of course, for choosing one as a sleuth. Her presence jars the ordinary convention and adds to the fun.

The air of mystery about nuns persists despite the fact that after the Second Vatican Council customs in convents changed dramatically. Gone, for the most part, are the cumbersome habits and restrictive rules. Many Sisters have returned to the use of their baptismal names, family names included.

Contrary to some prevailing misconceptions, the majority of women religious are well-educated, forceful, and courageous with very little, if anything, to conceal.

As women, they are accustomed to dealing with

the human condition and well able to understand human behavior. As religious, they are concerned, not only with holiness, good works and the needs of people, but they have a professional interest in sin and the sinner which makes them especially suited to solving crimes. Put their womanhood and their religious calling together and you come up with a dynamite combination for a series detective.

To be perfectly honest, however, what led me to choose a Sister sleuth for my own murder mysteries had nothing to do with any of these pluses. I chose a nun because I am a nun myself.

Having been a Sister for almost forty years, I have a pretty good grasp on how one thinks, feels and lives. Sometimes, I think that my readers find the authentic "bits of business" about convent life one of the main attractions in my books. But that's beside the point.

Because of my own life style, it seemed only logical that I choose a Sister for the protagonist in my series.

Deciding on a nun, however, had its limitations. My sleuth could not be extremely wealthy or pursue a devil-may-care career. She could not raise exotic animals, have an affair, however discreet, or even use four letter words. I needed an exceptional nun; one, above all, who by the very ordinariness of her life was not going to turn into a colossal bore.

My nun-sleuth needed to be old enough to be wise, yet young and adventurous in spirit. She must command respect without being stand-offish; must be learned without being a snob; witty without being flip. My nun must be one who understands human foibles without being judgmental or bitter. I wanted a nun who was unflappable, warm-hearted, salty yet lovable.

Most important, I wanted someone who would wear well.

Suddenly it occurred to me that I knew such a nun and had known her for nearly all of my religious life. Her name was Sister Mary Helen and she had been my first principal when I started to teach in 1954.

"Do you mind if I use your name and personality for a murder mystery I'm thinking of writing?" I asked her one day when I was doing just that, "thinking of writing."

She looked up from her reading—a paperback in the plastic prayerbook cover—shoved her bifocals up the bridge of her nose, and shrugged.

"Oh, go ahead, honey," she said with a wry smile. "I'll be dead long before you ever finish."

With that challenge, I went to work in earnest. I incorporated some of her expressions (like "pocketbook" and "how-do"), exaggerated her mannerisms, and even pirated a few of her friends. Before long, I hit on a stumbling block—her age.

"I know it's impolite to ask," I ventured one day, "but, you know, I really have no idea how old you are."

"Yes, it is impolite to ask," was the only answer I received, so I made her 76, hoping I was on the flattering side of reality.

When *Novena for Murder* was finally completed, I could not for the life of me persuade the real Mary Helen to read the manuscript. She was impressed when Scribner's Sons bought it, but still not impressed enough to read it.

Religious Detective Fiction: A Symposium 135

"Let's see what the critics say," was her excuse.

"It is, after all, only fiction," she remarked when the other nuns told her the critics liked Sister Mary Helen, sleuth.

Finally, she read my mystery.

"I don't mean to be critical," she said to me when she had finished, "but, you have a tendency to use 'old girl' and 'old dear' repeatedly. It slows down the action, comes across as a little condescending, and I'm afraid some older people may take offense."

Before *Novena for Murder* had been on the market for too long, Sister Mary Helen began to get into the spirit of the thing and joined me at a book signing.

"You'd better hurry," I said, signing books as quickly as I could, noticing a long line waiting for her.

"Not me, honey," she put down the felt pen, "I'm saving myself for the sequel."

Naturally, I hurried to finish *Advent of Dying*, the second Sister Mary Helen mystery, this time eliminating many of the "old girls" and "old dears." I didn't have as much trouble getting the real Sister Mary Helen to read it and she remarked that my omissions had improved the general quality of my writing!

Now, some people write to Sister Mary Helen, some actually call to speak to her. I have to explain that I am the author and she is, in part, a figment of my imagination.

When I told her about this, Mary Helen laughed.

"All my life, I have kept the Ten Commandments, the Six Precepts of the Church and my three vows. I have been a religious for over sixty years," she said, "and I never had so much attention until you wrote that dumb book."

I stewed about this for a couple of days, until the real Sister Mary Helen sent me a snapshot. In it, she and several politically active members of the Older Women's League (OWLS) were picketing the Federal Building for Social Security reforms.

Each woman held a large sign stating, "Honk if you love your mother."

"Now here is what someone should write about," she had penned on the back of the photo. And so I did, producing another Sister Mary Helen mystery, *The Missing Madonna.*

As I begin *Murder in Ordinary Time*, I am well aware that in picking my Sister sleuth, I did, indeed, pick a winner. Writing about Sister Mary Helen and her propensity for murder is one habit that I cannot seem to shed.

BIBLIOGRAPHY

(Edition listed is the first, followed by the first American if different. Works not available in English have not been included.)

I. Works of Fiction and Drama Referred to in the Essays

Alington, C.A. *Archdeacons Afloat.* London: Faber, 1946.

Allen, Woody. "Nefarious Times We Live In." In his *Side Effects.* New York: Random, 1980.

Appel, H.M. "Blood Feast," *Dime Mystery*, March 1935.

Baxt, George. *"I" Said the Demon.* New York: Random, 1967.

_____. *A Parade of Cockeyed Creatures.* New York: Random, 1967.

_____. *Satan Is a Woman.* New York: International Polygonics, 1987.

Bergman, Andrew. *The Big Kiss-Off of 1944.* New York: Holt, 1974.

_____. *Hollywood and LeVine.* New York: Holt, 1975.

Black, Veronica. *A Vow of Silence.* London: Hale; New York: St. Martin's, 1990.

Booth, Clare (Clare Booth Luce). *Margin for Error*. New York: Dramatists, 1940.

Burks, Arthur J. "Devils in the Dust," *Thrilling Mystery*, December 1935.

Burns, Rex. *The Avenging Angel*. New York: Viking, 1983.

Butler, John K. "The Saint in Silver," *Dime Detective*, January 1941.

Byfield, Barbara Ninde, and Frank L. Tedeschi. *Solemn High Murder*. Garden City, NY: Doubleday, 1975.

Catalan, Henri. *Soeur Angele and the Embarrassed Ladies*. New York: Sheed and Ward, 1955.

Cave, Hugh B. "School Mistress for the Mad," *Sinister Stories*, April 1940.

Chance, Stephen (Philip William Turner). *Septimus and the Danedyke Mystery*. London: Bodley, 1971. New York: Nelson, 1973.

Chesterton, G.K. "The Donnington Affair." *The Premier*, October and November 1914; reprinted in his *Thirteen Detectives*. Ed. Marie Smith. London: Xanadu; New York: Dodd, Mead, 1987.

_____. *The Incredulity of Father Brown*. London: Cassell; New York: Dodd, Mead, 1926.

_____. *The Innocence of Father Brown*. London: Cassell; New York: Lane, 1911.

_____. *The Man Who Was Thursday*. Bristol: Arrowsmith; New York: Dodd, Mead, 1908.

_____. *The Scandal of Father Brown.* London: Cassell; New York: Dodd, Mead, 1935.

_____. *The Secret of Father Brown.* London: Cassell; New York: Harper, 1927.

_____. *The Wisdom of Father Brown.* London: Cassell, 1914. New York: Lane, 1915.

Cook, Thomas H. *Tabernacle.* Boston: Houghton Mifflin, 1983.

Coxe, George Harmon. *The Groom Lay Dead.* New York: Knopf, 1944.

Davis, Dorothy Salisbury. *A Gentle Murderer.* New York: Scribners, 1951.

_____. *Where the Dark Streets Go.* New York: Scribners, 1969.

Delman, David. *He Who Digs a Grave.* Garden City, NY: Doubleday, 1973.

_____. *Murder in the Family.* Garden City, NY: Doubleday, 1985.

_____. *Sudden Death.* Garden City, NY: Doubleday, 1972.

Dewey, Thomas B. *The Love-Death Thing.* New York: Simon and Schuster, 1969.

Doyle, Arthur Conan. *The Land of Mist.* London: Hutchinson; New York: Doran, 1926.

_____. *A Study in Scarlet.* London: Beeton's Christmas Annual, 1887. Philadelphia: Lippincott, 1890.

Drummond, Ivor (Roger Longrigg). *The Priests of the Abomination*. London: Macmillan, 1970.

Eco, Umberto. *The Name of the Rose*. London: Secker; San Diego: Harcourt, Brace, Jovanovich, 1983.

Engel, Howard. *Murder on Location*. Toronto: Clarke, 1982. New York: St. Martin's, 1985.

_____. *Murder Sees the Light*. Markham, Ontario: Penguin, 1984. New York: St. Martin's, 1985.

_____. *The Ransom Game*. Toronto: Clarke, 1981. New York: St. Martin's, 1984.

_____. *The Suicide Murders*. Toronto: Clarke, 1980. New York: St. Martin's, 1984.

Ernst, Paul. "Devil at the Wheel," *Thrilling Mystery*, January 1936.

_____. "Man into Monster," *Terror Tales*, August 1935.

_____. "The Thing Behind the Iron Door," *Horror Stories*, October-November, 1937.

Fliegel, Richard. *The Next to Die*. New York: Bantam, 1986.

Forrest, Richard. *Lark*. New York: NAL, 1986.

Gault, William Campbell. *The Dead Seed*. New York: Walker, 1985.

Gray, Russell (Bruno Fischer). "Burn - Lovely Lady," *Dime Mystery*, June 1938.

———. "Plague of the Black Passion," *Horror Stories*, August-September 1939.

Greeley, Andrew M. *Angels of September.* New York: Warner, 1986.

———. *Happy Are the Meek.* New York: Warner, 1985.

———. *Happy Are the Clean of Heart.* New York: Warner, 1986.

———. *Happy Are Those Who Thirst for Justice.* New York: Mysterious, 1987.

———. *Patience of a Saint.* New York: Warner, 1986.

———. *Virgin and Martyr.* New York: Warner, 1985.

Greenburg, Dan. *Love Kills.* New York: Harcourt, Brace, Jovanovich, 1978.

Greenwood, John (John Buxton Hilton). *Mists Over Mosley.* New York: Walker, 1986.

Grisman, Arnold. *The Winning Streak.* New York: St. Martin's, 1985.

Hammett, Dashiell. *The Dain Curse.* New York: Knopf, 1929.

———. *Red Harvest.* New York: Knopf, 1929.

Haughey, Thomas Brace. *The Case of the Invisible Thief.* Minneapolis: Bethany, 1978.

———. *The Case of the Hijacked Moon.*

Minneapolis: Bethany, 1981.

Haymon, S.T. *Death and the Pregnant Virgin.* London: Constable; New York: St. Martin's, 1980.

_____. *Death of a God.* London: Constable; New York: St. Martin's, 1987.

_____. *Ritual Murder.* London: Constable; New York: St. Martin's, 1982.

_____. *Stately Homicide.* London: Constable; New York: St. Martin's, 1984.

_____. *A Very Particular Murder.* London: Constable; New York: St. Martin's, 1989.

Head, Matthew (John Canaday). *The Cabinda Affair.* New York: Simon and Schuster, 1949.

Himes, Chester. *Blind Man with a Pistol.* New York: Morrow, 1969.

Hirschberg, Cornelius. *Florentine Finish.* New York: Harper, 1963.

"The History of Bel." The Apocryphal Scriptures, reprinted in Dorothy L. Sayers, ed., *Great Short Stories of Detection, Mystery, and Horror.* London: Gollancz, 1928; as *The Omnibus of Crime*, New York: Payson, 1929.

"The History of Susanna." The Apocryphal Scriptures, reprinted in Dorothy L. Sayers, ed., *Great Short Stories of Detection, Mystery, and Horror.* London: Gollancz, 1928; as *The Omnibus of Crime*, New York: Payson, 1929.

Hoch, Edward D. "The Sweating Statue," in Frank D. McSherry, Jr., Martin H. Greenberg, and

Charles G. Waugh, eds., *Detectives A to Z*. New York: Bonanza, 1985.

_____. "Sword for a Sinner," *Saint Mystery Magazine*, October 1959.

_____. "The Vicar of Hell," *Famous Detective Stories*, August 1956.

_____. "Village of the Dead," *Famous Detective Stories*, December 1955.

_____. "The Way up to Hades," *Alfred Hitchcock's Mystery Magazine*, January, 1988.

Holland, Isabelle. *A Death at St. Anselm's*. Garden City, NY: Doubleday, 1984.

_____. *A Fatal Advent*. Garden City, NY: Doubleday, 1989.

Holton, Leonard (Leonard Wibberley). *Deliver Us from Wolves*. New York: Dodd, Mead, 1963.

_____. *The Devil to Play*. New York: Dodd, Mead, 1974.

_____. *A Pact with Satan*. New York: Dodd, Mead, 1960.

_____. *A Problem of Angels*. New York: Dodd, Mead, 1970.

_____. *The Saint Maker*. New York: Dodd, Mead, 1959.

_____. *Secret of the Doubting Saint*. New York: Dodd, Mead, 1961.

_____. *A Touch of Jonah*. New York: Dodd,

Mead, 1968.

Holmes, H.H. (Anthony Boucher). *Nine Times Nine.* New York: Duell, 1940.

_____. *Rocket to the Morgue.* New York: Duell, 1942.

_____. "The Stripper," *Ellery Queen's Mystery Magazine*, May 1945.

Irvine, Robert R. *The Angels' Share.* New York: St. Martin's, 1989.

_____. *Baptism for the Dead.* New York: Dodd, Mead, 1988.

_____. *Gone to Glory.* New York: St. Martin's, 1990.

Jevons, Marshall. *The Fatal Equilibrium.* Cambridge: MIT, 1985.

_____. *Murder at the Margin.* Sun Lakes, AZ: Horton, 1978.

Johnson, James L. *Code Name Sebastian.* Philadelphia: Lippincott, 1967.

Jones, Cleo. *Prophet Motive.* New York: St. Martin's, 1984.

Kane, Frank. *Poisons Unknown.* New York: Washburn, 1953.

Kaye, Marvin. *My Brother, the Druggist.* Garden City, NY: Doubleday, 1979.

_____. *My Son, the Druggist.* Garden City, NY: Doubleday, 1977.

Bibliography

Kellerman, Faye. *Milk and Honey.* New York: Morrow, 1990.

_____. *The Quality of Mercy.* New York: Morrow, 1989.

_____. *The Ritual Bath.* New York: Arbor, 1986.

_____. *Sacred and Profane.* New York: Arbor, 1987.

Kellerman, Jonathan. *Blood Test.* New York: Atheneum, 1986.

_____. *The Butcher's Theater.* New York: Bantam, 1988.

Kemelman, Harry. *Conversations with Rabbi Small.* New York: Morrow, 1981.

_____. *Friday the Rabbi Slept Late.* New York: Crown, 1964.

_____. *Monday the Rabbi Took Off.* New York: Putnam, 1972.

_____. *The Nine Mile Walk.* New York: Putnam, 1967.

_____. *One Fine Day the Rabbi Bought a Cross.* New York: Morrow, 1987.

_____. *Saturday the Rabbi Went Hungry.* New York: Crown, 1966.

_____. *Someday the Rabbi Will Leave.* New York: Morrow, 1985.

_____. *Sunday the Rabbi Stayed Home.* New

York: Putnam, 1969.

_____. *Thursday the Rabbi Walked Out.* New York: Morrow, 1978.

_____. *Tuesday the Rabbi Saw Red.* New York: Fields, 1974.

_____. *Wednesday the Rabbi Got Wet.* New York: Morrow, 1976.

Kienzle, William X. *Assault with Intent.* Kansas City: Andrews and McMeel, 1982.

_____. *Deadline for a Critic.* Kansas City: Andrews and McMeel, 1987.

_____. *Death Wears a Red Hat.* Kansas City: Andrews and McMeel, 1980.

_____. *Eminence.* Kansas City: Andrews and McMeel, 1989.

_____. *Kill and Tell.* Kansas City: Andrews and McMeel, 1984.

_____. *Masquerade.* Kansas City: Andrews and McMeel, 1990.

_____. *Mind Over Murder.* Kansas City: Andrews and McMeel, 1981.

_____. *The Rosary Murders.* Kansas City: Andrews and McMeel, 1979.

_____. *Shadow of Death.* Kansas City: Andrews and McMeel, 1983.

_____. *Sudden Death.* Kansas City: Andrews and McMeel, 1985.

Larsen, Gaylord. *Atascadero Island.* New York: Ballantine, 1989.

_____. *Dorothy and Agatha.* New York: Dutton, 1990.

_____. *The Kilbourne Connection.* Minneapolis: Bethany, 1980.

_____. *The 180-Degree Murder.* New York: Ballantine, 1987.

_____. *A Paramount Kill.* New York: Dutton, 1988.

_____. *Trouble Crossing the Pyrenees.* Ventura, CA: Regal, 1983.

Lockridge, Richard. *The Old Die Young.* Philadelphia: Lippincott, 1980.

_____. *--Or Was He Pushed.* Philadelphia: Lippincott, 1975.

_____. *Preach No More.* Philadelphia: Lippincott, 1971.

_____. *A Streak of Light.* Philadelphia: Lippincott, 1976.

_____. *Write Murder Down.* Philadelphia: Lippincott, 1972.

Love, William F. *The Chartreuse Clue.* New York: Fine, 1990.

Lyons, Arthur. *All God's Children.* New York: Mason/Charter, 1975.

McConnell, Frank. *Murder Among Friends.* New York: Walker, 1983.

MacDonald, John D. *The Green Ripper.* Philadelphia: Lippincott, 1979.

Macdonald, John (Ross) (Kenneth Millar). *The Moving Target.* New York: Knopf, 1949.

McInerny, Ralph. *Bishop as Pawn.* New York: Vanguard, 1978.

_____. *Four on the Floor.* New York: St. Martin's, 1989.

_____. *Getting a Way with Murder.* New York: Vanguard, 1984.

_____. *The Grass Widow.* New York: Vanguard, 1983.

_____. *Her Death of Cold.* New York: Vanguard, 1977.

_____. *Lying Three.* New York: Vanguard, 1979.

_____. *Second Vespers.* New York: Vanguard, 1980.

_____. *The Seventh Station.* New York: Vanguard, 1979.

_____. *Thicker Than Water.* New York: Vanguard, 1981.

McNamara, Joseph. *The First Directive.* New York: Crown, 1984.

Marsh, Ngaio. *Death in Ecstasy.* London: Bles, 1936. New York: Sheridan, 1941.

_____. *Spinsters in Jeopardy.* Boston: Little, Brown, 1953.

Mason, A.E.W. *The Prisoner in the Opal.* London: Hodder; Garden City, NY: Doubleday, 1928.

Merritt, A. *Seven Footprints to Satan.* New York: Boni, 1928.

Millar, Margaret. *How Like an Angel.* New York: Random, 1962.

Nevins, Francis M., Jr. *The Ninety-Million-Dollar Mouse.* New York: Walker, 1987.

O'Marie, Sister Carol Anne. *A Novena for Murder.* New York: Scribners, 1984.

_____. *Advent of Dying.* New York: St. Martin's, 1986.

_____. *The Missing Madonna.* New York: Delacorte, 1988.

Peters, Ellis (Edith Parteger). *Dead Man's Ransom.* London: Macmillan, 1984. New York: Morrow, 1985.

_____. *The Devil's Novice.* London: Macmillan, 1983. New York: Morrow, 1984.

_____. *The Heretic's Apprentice.* London: Headline, 1989. New York: Mysterious, 1990.

_____. *The Leper of St. Giles.* London: Macmillan, 1981. New York: Morrow, 1982.

_____. *Monk's Hood.* London: Macmillan, 1980.

New York: Morrow, 1981.

_____. *A Morbid Taste for Bones.* London: Macmillan, 1977. New York: Morrow, 1978.

_____. *The Potter's Field.* London: Headline, 1989. New York: Mysterious, 1990.

_____. *The Virgin in the Ice.* London: Macmillan, 1982. New York: Morrow, 1983.

Post, Melville Davisson. *The Complete Uncle Abner.* Del Mar, CA: UC San Diego Extension, 1977.

_____. *The Methods of Uncle Abner.* Boulder, CO: Aspen, 1974.

_____. *Uncle Abner, Master of Mysteries.* New York: Appleton, 1918.

Prather, Richard S. *Always Leave 'em Dying.* Greenwich, CT: Gold Medal, 1954.

_____. *Dead-Bang.* New York: Pocket, 1965.

_____. *Dead Man's Walk.* New York: Pocket, 1965.

Queen, Ellery. *And on the Eighth Day.* New York: Random, 1964.

_____. *The Egyptian Cross Mystery.* New York: Stokes, 1932.

Quill, Monica (Ralph McInerny). *And Then There Was Nun.* New York: Vanguard, 1984.

_____. *Let Us Prey.* New York: Vanguard, 1982.

Bibliography

———. *Not a Blessed Thing.* New York: Vanguard, 1981.

———. *Nun of the Above.* New York: Vanguard, 1985.

———. *Sine Qua Nun.* New York: Vanguard, 1986.

———. *The Veil of Ignorance.* New York: St. Martin's, 1988.

Quinn, Seabury. *The Devil's Bride.* New York: Popular Library, 1976.

Randisi, Robert J. *Eye in the Ring.* New York: Avon, 1982.

———. *The Steinway Collection.* New York: Avon, 1983.

Rawson, Clayton. *Death from a Top Hat.* New York: Putnam, 1938.

Reach, Alice Scanlan. "In the Confessional," *Ellery Queen's Mystery Magazine,* June 1982.

———. "The Ordeal of Father Crumlish," *Ellery Queen's Mystery Magazine,* April 1963.

Resnicow, Herbert. *The Gold Deadline.* New York: St. Martin's, 1984.

———. *The Gold Frame.* New York: St. Martin's, 1985.

———. *The Gold Solution.* New York: St. Martin's, 1983.

Rogers, Wayne. "Tomorrow They Die," *Mystery Adventures*, March 1935.

Rosen, R.D. *Fadeaway*. New York: Harper, 1986.

_____. *Strike Three, You're Dead*. New York: Walker, 1984.

Rosten, Leo. *Silky!* New York: Harper, 1979.

Sale, Richard B. "Rescued by Satan," *Mystery Adventures*, May 1936.

Schachner, Nat. "Monsters of the Pit," *Terror Tales*, November 1934.

Scherf, Margaret. *Always Murder a Friend*. Garden City, NY: Doubleday, 1948.

Schorr, Mark. *Ace of Diamonds*. New York: St. Martin's, 1984.

_____. *Diamond Rock*. New York: St. Martin's, 1985.

_____. *Red Diamond, Private Eye*. New York: St. Martin's, 1983.

Shannon, Dell (Elizabeth Linington). *Extra Kill*. New York: Morrow, 1962.

Shepherd, Eric. *More Murder in a Nunnery*. New York: Sheed and Ward, 1954.

_____. *Murder in a Nunnery*. New York: Sheed and Ward, 1940.

Simon, Roger L. *The Big Fix*. San Francisco: Straight Arrow, 1973.

Bibliography

_____. *California Roll.* New York: Villard, 1985.

_____. *Peking Duck.* New York: Simon and Schuster, 1979.

_____. *Raising the Dead.* New York: Villard, 1988.

_____. *The Straight Man.* New York: Villard, 1986.

_____. *Wild Turkey.* San Francisco: Straight Arrow, 1975.

Smith, Charles Merrill. *Reverend Randollph and the Avenging Angel.* New York: Putnam, 1977.

_____. *Reverend Randollph and the Fall from Grace, Inc.* New York: Putnam: 1978.

_____. *Reverend Randollph and the Splendid Samaritan.* New York: Putnam, 1986.

_____. *Reverend Randollph and the Unholy Bible.* New York: Putnam, 1983.

_____. *Reverend Randollph and the Wages of Sin.* New York: Putnam, 1974.

Smith, J.C.S. *Jacoby's First Case.* New York: Atheneum, 1980.

_____. *Nightcap.* New York: Atheneum, 1984.

Smith, Julie. *Tourist Trap.* New York: Mysterious, 1986.

Smith, Terrence Lore. *Reverend Randollph and the Modern Miracles.* New York: Putnam, 1988.

Steward, Gary. *The Tenth Virgin.* New York: St. Martin's, 1983.

———. *The Zarahemla Vision.* New York: St. Martin's, 1986.

———. "The Foot-Washing Baptist," *Black Mask,* 1926.

Suter, J. Paul. "The Problem of the Man Who Sowed the Wind," *Black Mask,* August 1926.

Telushkin, Joseph. *The Final Analysis of Dr. Stark.* New York: Bantam, 1988.

———. *The Unorthodox Murder of Rabbi Wahl.* New York: Bantam, 1987.

Walsh, John Evangelist. *The Man Who Buried Jesus.* New York: Collier/Macmillan, 1989.

Ward, Frank. "The Dark Corner," *Mike Shayne Mystery Magazine,* January 1959, reprinted in Herr/Wells anthology (see below).

Warriner, Thurman. *Method in His Murder.* London: Hodder; New York: Macmillan, 1950.

Watson, Colin. *Broomsticks Over Flaxborough.* London: Eyre, 1972. U.S. edition as *Kissing Covens.* New York: Putnam, 1972.

Webb, Jack. *The Big Sin.* New York: Rinehart, 1952.

———. *The Brass Halo.* New York: Rinehart, 1957.

———. *The Deadly Sex.* New York: Rinehart, 1959.

Bibliography

Wheatley, Dennis. *The Devil Rides Out.* London: Hutchinson, 1935.

_____. *Gunmen, Gallants, and Ghosts.* London: Hutchinson, 1943.

_____. *The Satanist.* London: Hutchinson, 1960. New York: Ballantine, 1974.

_____. *To the Devil a Daughter.* London: Hutchinson, 1953.

Whitechurch, Victor L. *The Crime at Diana's Pool.* London: Unwin; New York: Duffield, 1927.

Wolk, Michael. *The Big Picture.* New York: Signet, 1985.

Woolrich, Cornell. "Baal's Daughter," *Thrilling Mystery*, January 1936.

_____. "Dark Melody of Death," *Dime Mystery*, July 1935.

_____. "Graves for the Living," *Dime Mystery*, June 1973.

_____. "Holocaust," *Argosy*, December 12, 1936.

_____. "Vampire's Honeymoon," *Horror Stories*, August-September, 1939.

Yaffe, James. *Mom Meets Her Maker.* New York: St. Martin's, 1990.

_____. *A Nice Murder for Mom.* New York: St. Martin's, 1988.

II. Anthologies

Herr, Dan, and Joel Wells, eds. *Bodies and Souls.* Garden City, NY: Doubleday, 1961.

Hoch, Edward D., and Martin H. Greenberg, eds. *Murder Most Sacred: Great Catholic Tales of Mystery and Suspense.* New York: Dembner, 1989.

III. Secondary Sources

Aird, Catherine. "The Devout: Benefit of Clergy." In Dilys Winn, ed. *Murder Ink.* New York: Workman, 1977, 467-469.

Browne, Ray. "Sherlock Holmes as Christian Detective: *The Case of the Invisible Thief.*" In his *Heroes and Humanities: Detective Fiction and Culture.* Bowling Green: Bowling Green State U. Popular P., 1986, 127-133.

Cleary, Maryell. "Contemporary Clergy-Detectives." *The Mystery Fancier*, 9 (May-June 1987): 3-21.

"Divine Mysteries." Special issue of *Mystery Readers of America Journal*, 3 (Spring 1987): 1-31.

Holton, Leonard. "Father Bredder." In Otto Penzler, ed. *The Great Detectives.* Boston: Little, 1978, 27-35.

Keating, H.R.F. "Brown Studies." In his *The Bedside Companion to Crime.* London: O'Mara; New York: Mysterious, 1989, 82, 84-88.

Rosenberger, Edgar S. "The Religious Sherlock Holmes." *The Baker Street Journal*, April 1948, reprinted in Philip A. Shreffler, ed. *Sherlock*

Holmes by Gas-Lamp: Highlights from the First Four Decades of the Baker Street Journal. New York: Fordham UP, 1989, 48-57.

Routley, Erik. *The Puritan Pleasures of the Detective Story: A Personal Monograph.* London: Gollancz, 1972.

Spencer, William David. *Mysterium and Mystery: The Clerical Crime Novel.* (Studies in Religion, No. 6.) Ann Arbor: UMI, 1989.

Tracy, Jack. *Conan Doyle and the Latter-Day Saints.* Revised and expanded edition. Bloomington, IN: Gaslight, 1979.

INDEX OF NAMES

Abbott, Anthony, vi
Alington, C.A., 58, 59
Allen, Woody, 105
Anthelme, Paul, 1
Apple, H.M., 87
Auden, W.H., 21, 47
Austen, Jane, 24, 26
Baker, Ivon, v
Bakker, Jim, vii
Baxt, George, 47, 48
Bergman, Andrew, 32, 33, 34
Black, Veronica, 17
Bogart, Humphrey, 34
Boucher, Anthony, vi, 4, 5, 6, 13, 95, 96
Bourde, Paul, 1
Browne, Ray B., 70
Burks, Arthur J., 89
Burns, Rex, 114
Butler, John K., 96
Byfield, Barbara Ninde, 59
Canaday, John, 59
Catalan, Henri, 7
Cave, Hugh B., 87
Chance, Stephen, 59
Chandler, Raymond, 32, 54
Chesterton, G.K., vi, 1, 2, 3, 4, 5, 16, 30, 57, 70
Cleary, Maryell, vi, 68
Cook, Thomas H., 115
Coward, Noel, 83
Coxe, George Harmon, 93, 94

Crispin, Edmund, vi
Dannay, Frederic, 22, 31
Davis, Dorothy Salisbury, 5, 6
Delman, David, 39, 40, 42, 43
Dewey, Thomas B., 105
Doyle, Arthur Conan, vi, 111, 112, 113
Eco, Umberto, 16
Engel, Howard, 36, 37, 38
Ernst, Paul, 87
Falwell, Jerry, vii
Fischer, Bruno, 88, 89
Fliegel, Richard, 30
Ford, Gerald, 104
Forrest, Richard, 94
Friedman, Milton, 44
Gault, William Campbell, 106
Gilbert, Michael, vi
Gordon, Gordon, vi
Gordon, Mildred, vi
Gray, Russell, 88, 89
Greeley, Andrew M., v, 14
Greenberg, Martin H., 9, 16
Greenburg, Dan, 31
Greenwood, John, 84
Griffith, D.W., 111
Grisman, Arnold, 31
Hammett, Dashiell, 22, 54, 85, 98

Haughey, Thomas Brace, 70
Haymon, S.T., 50, 51, 52, 53, 55
Head, Matthew, 59
Herr, Dan, 8
Himes, Chester, 95
Hirschberg, Cornelius, 46
Hitchcock, Alfred, 1
Hoch, Edward D., vi, vii, 9, 16, 101, 102, 103
Holland, Isabelle, 59, 77
Holmes, H.H., 4, 95
Holton, Leonard, 7, 11
Hubin, Allen J., 70
Hughes, Dorothy B., vi
Irvine, Robert, 121, 122, 123
Jevons, Marshall, 44
Johnson, James L., 59
Jones, Cleo, 118, 120
Kane, Frank, 91
Kaye, Marvin, 47, 49, 50
Keating, H.R.F., 60
Kellerman, Faye, vi, 29, 30, 55
Kellerman, Jonathan, vi, 55, 107, 108
Kemelman, Harry, viii, 8, 23, 24, 25, 26, 27, 29, 57, 68, 70, 127, 130, 131
Kienzle, William X., v, vi, 4, 10, 11, 12, 17, 127, 128, 129, 130
Knox, Ronald, v, 4
Lachman, Marvin, viii
Larsen, Gaylord, viii, 60, 70, 71, 72, 73, 74, 77
Lathen, Emma, 63

Lee, Manfred, 22, 31
Lewis, Jerry, 50
Lewis, Sinclair, 24, 26
Lockridge, Frances, 37
Lockridge, Richard, 37, 38, 39
Love, William F., 17
Lyons, Arthur, 30, 105
MacDonald, John D., 108, 109, 115
MacDonald, Ross, 54, 97
Marsh, Ngaio, 80, 81, 95
Mason, A.E.W., 79, 80
Maugham, Somerset, 106
McConnell, Frank, 13
McInerny, Ralph, vi, 9, 12, 13, 17, 130
McNamara, Joseph, 108
McSherry, Frank D., Jr., 9
Merritt, A., 85
Millar, Kenneth, 97
Millar, Margaret, 100
Nevins, Francis M., 103
Nevins, Francis M., Jr, 9
Nixon, Richard, 33
O'Marie, Sister Carol Anne, v, viii, 13, 127, 131
Orwell, George, 21
Oursler, Fulton, vi
Pargeter, Edith, 15
Pemberton, Max, 16
Peters, Ellis, viii, 15, 17, 127, 128, 129, 130
Post, Melville Davisson, 22, 58
Prather, Richard S., 91, 97, 98, 99

Index

Queen, Ellery, vi, 22, 55, 92, 101
Quill, Monica, 12, 13
Quinn, Seabury, 84, 85
Randisi, Robert J., 31
Rawson, Clayton, 92, 93
Reach, Alice Scanlan, 8
Resnicow, Herbert, 47, 49
Robertson, Pat, vii
Rogers, Wayne, 89
Rosen, R.D., 44, 45
Rosenberger, Edgar S., vi
Rosten, Leo, 47, 48
Routely, Erik, vi
Runyon, Damon 31
Sale, Richard B., 90
Sayers, Dorothy L., v, vi
Schachner, Nat, 89
Scherf, Margaret, 59
Schorr, Mark, 30
Shannon, Dell, 100
Shepherd, Eric, 7
Simon, Roger L., 34, 35, 36, 55, 104
Smith, Charles Merrill, v, viii, 65, 60, 66, 68, 69, 70
Smith, Terrence Lore, 66, 67, 68
Spencer, William David, vi, 58, 69
Stewart, Gary, 116
Suter, J. Paul, 57
Swaggart, Jimmy, vii
Tedeschi, Frank L., 59
Telushkin, Joseph, v, 27, 28, 55
Tracy, Jack, 113, 114
Turner, Philip, 59

Walsh, John Evangelist, 70
Ward, Frank, 8
Washer, Robert, vi
Watson, Colin, 21, 83
Waugh, Charles G., 9
Webb, Jack, 6
Wells, Joel, 8
Wheatley, Dennis, 81, 82
Whitechurch, Victor L., v, 58
Wibberley, Leonard, 7
Wolk, Michael, 31
Wollrich, Cornell, 87, 88, 90
Yaffe, James, vii, 54, 55
Young, Brigham, 112, 113, 114, 115, 118, 124